"*The Gloomy Girl Variety Show* has everything I could ever want in a book. Dazzling, darkly funny, and fiercely incisive, Freda Epum takes center stage to deliver her profound insights on mental health, diaspora, belonging, and her search for home in a fragmented world. A masterful showman, Epum invites readers in with an honesty and heartfelt vulnerability that lingers long after the final word. These essays blew me away. I love *The Gloomy Girl Variety Show*, and you will too."

—**EDGAR GOMEZ**, author of
High-Risk Homosexual: A Memoir

"Reckoning with identity, illness, and in-betweenness, Freda Epum's voice comes through these pages like a flame: crackling with insight, wryly humorous even as it sears, and impossible to look away from. This hybrid marvel of a book is not just a variety show but a magic show—you will be transformed."

—**ERICA BERRY**, author of *Wolfish: Wolf, Self,*
and the Stories We Tell About Fear

"*The Gloomy Girl Variety Show* is a one-of-a-kind, thought-provoking tour of contemporary American life. Knitting vignettes to poetry and photography, this memoir urges us to reconsider how we think and talk about mental health, pop culture, and Black women's lives. Whether chronicling 'How to Be a Terrible No-Good African Daughter' or testifying on 'Why (I Choose to Remember),' Freda Epum writes with tenderness and great wit. She is a vibrant new voice for our times."

—**DAISY HERNÁNDEZ**, author of *The Kissing Bug:*
A True Story of a Family, an Insect, and a
Nation's Neglect of a Deadly Disease

THE
GLOOMY GIRL
VARIETY SHOW

A MEMOIR

FREDA EPUM

THE FEMINIST PRESS
AT THE CITY UNIVERSITY OF NEW YORK
NEW YORK CITY

Published in 2025 by the Feminist Press
at the City University of New York
The Graduate Center
365 Fifth Avenue, Suite 5406
New York, NY 10016

feministpress.org

First Feminist Press edition 2025

 This book is made possible by the New York State Council
on the Arts with the support of the Office of the Governor
and the New York State Legislature.

The epigraph on page v from "Writing about Housing Anxiety in the Contemporary Novel" by Laura Maw, copyright © 2021 by Laura Maw, is used by permission of the author.

The epigraph on page v from *Beloved* by Toni Morrison, copyright © 1987 by Toni Morrison, is used by permission of Alfred A. Knopf, an imprint of the Knopf Doubleday Publishing Group, a division of Penguin Random House LLC.

The epigraph on page v from "Theory as Liberatory Practice" by bell hooks, copyright © 1991 by the *Yale Journal of Law and Feminism*, is used by permission of the *Yale Journal of Law and Feminism*.

First printing January 2025

Cover design by Dana Li
Cover art by Yasmin Idris
Text design by Drew Stevens

Library of Congress Cataloging-in-Publication Data
Names: Epum, Freda, author.
Title: The gloomy girl variety show : a memoir / Freda Epum.
Description: First Feminist Press edition. | New York City : The Feminist
   Press at the City University of New York, 2025.
Identifiers: LCCN 2024026704 (print) | LCCN 2024026705 (ebook) | ISBN
   9781558613102 (paperback) | ISBN 9781558613300 (ebook)
Subjects: LCSH: Epum, Freda. | Authors, American–21st century–Biography.
   | African American women–Biography. | Women with
   disabilities–Biography. | LCGFT: Autobiographies.
Classification: LCC PS3605.P86 Z46 2025 (print) | LCC PS3605.P86 (ebook)
   | DDC 814/.6 [B]–dc23/eng/20240830
LC record available at https://lccn.loc.gov/2024026704
LC ebook record available at https://lccn.loc.gov/2024026705

*Who can afford (or is afforded) a home, a
sense of permanence?*

*—Laura Maw, "Writing about
Housing Anxiety in the Contemporary Novel"*

*Shivering, Denver approached the house,
regarding it, as she always did, as a person
rather than a structure. A person that wept,
sighed, trembled and fell into fits.*

—Toni Morrison, Beloved

*"I came to theory because I was hurting—
the pain within me was so intense that I
could not go on living. I came to theory
desperate, wanting to comprehend—to
grasp what was happening around and
within me. Most importantly, I wanted to
make the hurt go away. I saw in theory then
a location for healing."*

*—bell hooks,
"Theory as Liberatory Practice"*

For
the ones from a no-place

Contents

Freda Epum, *Diary of a Wet Cloud Series*, 2015.
Image courtesy of Freda Epum.

INTRODUCTION:
HOUSE HUNTER

Forever Home

I dream of being on HGTV's *House Hunters*.

Of course, that's not happening because I am, like so many millennials, plagued by student loan debt. My middle-class income and meager savings won't buy me a house. But I need to tell you something. I've been searching for a home nevertheless for quite some time.

The realtor asks for my thoughts on location and architectural style. I tell her the interior is the most important to me. She shows me a few options, and I turn my focus to a one-bedroom with original wood floors, a lush backyard, and a new dishwasher. I confide in the realtor the stakes of this house hunt. I tell her that all my life I've mumbled the words "I want to go home," after a stressful day, a psychotic break, an argument with my mother. I want to go home, and I've never found it. I am looking for the forever home that I hear white people talk about on *Love It or List It*. If she can find me forever, I am sold.

Forever is a new concept for me.

That's not true.

I knew I wanted a forever when I was deeply depressed. I experienced my fair share of mental-health struggles during college and graduate school. As a tireless researcher, I intend to find the cure to my weeping.

No matter my current place of residence, my identities follow me. I've told you I'm searching, that I'm on the market for belonging. I want to inhabit renovated spaces, to establish a sense of home.

I was born in the desert city of Tucson, Arizona, to Nigerian parents. For most of my life, I've straddled two countries. Far from the ideal African daughter, I am an artist and writer. Throughout years of family strife, I've moved away, fallen in love (many times), and become sick.

I knew I wanted forever when I took those seven pills of Klonopin. I knew I wanted forever when I tried to drown myself. I knew I wanted forever, but my forever was pitch-black. For me, there was nothing on the other side.

If you can hold my story in your hands, maybe that means I'll be held forever.

My wish list: a fully furnished home with a great stove to cook family recipes, large windows to look out at the landscape, a couch to fall asleep on, a bed to lie in for hours, a bathtub to soak my pain away.

"Can you tell me more about the neighborhood?" I ask once the realtor and I settle on a few listings to see.

She shows me three houses, describing each one.

Freda Epum, *Diary of a Wet Cloud Series*, 2015.
Image courtesy of Sol Kim.

HOUSE #1:

THE FALLING-APART FOREIGNER FARMHOUSE

Allow me to take you on my literary revue. Theater is "playing make-believe," otherwise known as "playing house." Let us "play house"; let me take you on my House Hunt, reader. Let me set the stage for the worries of my mind—my womanhood, my otherness, my sickness, my foreignness, my Blackness. Worry. Worry. Worry. Other. Other. Other.

(Broken) Tongue

I look up phrases that are used to describe me. I write down words that I cannot pronounce. Speak but don't speak. Say but can't articulate. I am coming home to no one.

"Nigerian Pidgin English": a term for the blending of many Nigerian languages (primarily Igbo, Yoruba, and Hausa) and English. My parents exist on a bridge straddling two countries. They call me and my siblings Americans as a cheeky insult. Many Nigerians of my parents' generation aren't sure how to write their own language. This is also true for me.

For you to fully understand my crisis of identity, I must speak with "special intensity given to the expression of feelings and ideas."[1] I must perform what resembles a poem to tell you the gloomiest story of isolation. Isolation that makes clear the lack of "a place where something flourishes, is most typically found, or from which it originates."[2] I am without my own definition of home.

I enter the threshold and there I see you, this otherworldly body welcoming me. You're a manifestation of my dreams—dreams of distant lands. Dreams of me running and searching for home. They say that your dreams reveal your innermost thoughts, tell you of a you that is not given to the world—a you who hides. But here I am, here you are—skin and bone, earthworm and falcon.

I want to tell a story of you. Not about you. Something larger, something grander than saying, "Have you met the Atlantic? She's great." I want to tell a story of you. I want to express the relationship between a part and a whole. The sleeve of this coat. The breathing of fresh air. The rays of the sun. The merging of my two selves.

1. *Oxford English Dictionary Online*, s.v. "poetry," accessed April 19, 2024, https://www.oed.com/dictionary/poetry_n.
2. *Oxford English Dictionary Online*, s.v. "home," accessed April 19, 2024, https://www.oed.com/dictionary/home_n1.

The African Dream

I'm watching TV with my dad. *House Hunters* is on. We sit together on a tattered leather couch in a four-bedroom house with two and a half baths, eagerly awaiting the reveal of a much larger home with granite countertops and crown molding. Casually my dad tells me about the hut he used to live in while a commercial for *Tiny House Nation* flashes on-screen. How distant I feel from the life I would've had but will never know. A life of electricity that comes and goes, a life of my mother fetching water for her grandmother to take a shower, a life of cars that don't obey four-way stops, a life of pink doily dresses and braids too tight, done every six weeks or so.

We moved from our small house in a less desirable area of Tucson to a large house outside the city. It was around the time I turned eight years old. The dusty desert air smelled like the early aughts—chubby cheeks, skateboards, yellow school buses, Otter Pops. Wood became walls, became bedrooms, became memories, became nightmares. I took pictures with my siblings in front of the structure that would become another salmon-colored adobe house in a sea of salmon-colored adobe houses within a gated community outside Tucson.

I look out the window and see a vision of my mother sitting in her high school dorm room in Nigeria, surrounded by trendy clothing, posters, hair products, and lotions. She sits without smiling, unusual for her then but a habitual pose now. In the evenings, I daydream of another life in Nigeria, picturing every detail. I'm wearing a frilly lace shirt with Ankara fabric, and I can taste the jollof and shea butter and sweat in the air that my dad says engulfs you as you step off the plane.

This period of imaginary Africanization fixes me. It rebuilds me from broken, remolds my tongue, deconstructs the Atlantic. I zigzag against the current of the borderlands, never arriving.

I wrap my hair in a gele with golden aso oke fabric, textured and glossy. I sip on Heineken, hoping the beer will change my voice from meek to boisterous. Hoping it will transform me into someone who likes Heineken.

As a little girl, I stole my dad's wicker hat and pretended to be on a safari because the American school system told me all about *the country* of Africa. They shrunk down my continent until I could fit it into my pocket, muddying my white flower dress with its rich pigment, shades of brown like church doors and my father's suits. I colored the walls with brown Crayola to create mirrors of other selves.

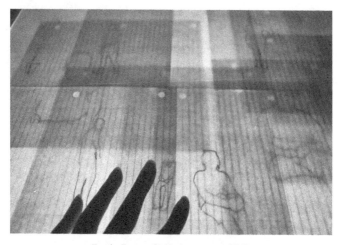

Freda Epum, *Body Language*, 2015.
Image courtesy of Freda Epum.

My father would sit me down every Easter to tell me fables of Jesus. I grabbed the glasses from his nose, adjusting my collar as if I was wearing a tie. I played with makeup and donned gold hoops, wondering when these costumes would become markers of my new identity.

My father told me proverbs. "Free, where are you going? Remember this." My siblings and I joked, making our voices deep like his baritone. "Let me tell you a story," we mimicked while wagging our fingers.

Later in adulthood, he told me about the time he flew from LaGuardia Airport in New York, and I told him about the time I almost got robbed there. My mother was cooking in the kitchen. Jollof rice or egusi. This might all be over in the next decade or two, or even a few years' time. I am reminded of Richard Fung's words in *My Mother's Place*: "My mother connects me to a past I would have no other way of knowing. And in this sea of whiteness, of friends, enemies, and strangers, I look at her and know who I am."[3]

My mother in her Nigerian accent pronounces the letter *h* "hey-ch" with a strong emphasis on the consonant. As a child, I would sleep in a bed with my sister when my room was taken over by family members on Thanksgiving. I'd lie in the dark after our late-night conversations and feel a pain in my side. It's funny how mental stress can cause physical pain. I feel a pain of not having, a pain of not knowing who I am in the world of West Africa, a pain deeper than I can explain. I'd say, "But I don't have an accent." Wishing that I could connect with my mother on the xenophobia she endures. We are both born two of everything—twoness of cultures, twoness of foreign and not foreign, twoness of pain in not knowing and pain in not having.

3. *My Mother's Place*, directed by Richard Fung (Video Data Bank: 1990), https://www.vdb.org/titles/my-mothers-place.

If I were to be a model daughter of an Igbo family, I would be holding a baby—six pounds, twelve ounces—its face tilted as I cradle its small head and tush. The air smelling of African sweat and mashed yams. I would be twenty-four years old with my firstborn child, just like my mother. I wonder what happens to the souls of mothers who have sacrificed themselves for their children's success. I wonder what happened to my mother's soul when she arrived in the United States, too foreign for this place. I wonder what happened to her soul as she uttered goodbye to her country. I wonder whether she cried the entire flight.

Did You Finish?

On Tuesdays Mary went to therapy.

"Are you sure you don't want to go to counseling again?" she texted me.

Mary was my best friend and the epitome of health and wellness. She went to spin class on Wednesdays, rock climbing on Thursdays, and Zumba on Fridays. On Mondays she did tantric meditation. On Saturdays she had date nights with her husband. On Sundays, brunch with her mother. She could usually squeeze me in sometime after brunch.

The tantric meditation craze had spread. Now my counseling sessions often involved me ranting about the week ahead and my old therapist Dr. Stein's parting words: "Your vagina is full of light."

It's not that I thought I didn't need therapy. I'd had enough of my mother's insistence that Africans didn't need therapy. "You don't want them to call you crazy," my mother would say. "All you need are proverbs and God." But my on-again, off-again relationship with God had ended years ago, so I tried my hand at therapy and had been working with Dr. Stein.

I knew the drill. Anxiety worksheets where you would write down your negative thoughts and cognitive distortions, then locate positive thoughts. All-or-nothing thinking, no one wants me, and then, magically—I guess I'm okay. I carried a notebook around with me for the first year of therapy and fired Dr. Stein after she handed me a flyer for tantric meditation.

I didn't think my glow-in-the-dark vagina would end my nightmares.

While in the waiting room to see Dr. Brown—my new therapist after Mary's insistence—I played a game guessing what the deal was with his other patients. It was mean, and I didn't care. There was the 6′4″ guy with the handlebar mustache who sat against the wall—combat PTSD. There was the red-haired girl whose hair hid her face as she snapped her wrist with a rubber band—self-harm. The fidgety guy who snuck in a few too many hits from his Juul vape pen—recovering from substance-abuse disorder.

Miss? The doctor will see you now.

I walked into an office with inspirational posters on the wall. One had a photograph of a man climbing steps like he was Rocky with "SUCCESS" stamped in giant yellow letters across the bottom.

Dr. Brown smiled a big toothy smile that was supposed to build rapport and put me at ease but only added to my discomfort. His face was pale and dotted with age spots, but he had a youthful haircut where the sides were taken in and there was more hair at the top. His green eyes were speckled with brown, like age spots. He told me to sit even though I was already seated. He asked if I felt sad, blue, and unhappy.

I smirked. "Just a little, quite a lot, and very much."

Now, Miss, I just want to do a short diagnostic exam so that we can get to know each other a bit. Let's get started.

do you worry have you lost control over do you worry how much do you eat do you feel worry feel sad down hopeless are you troubled repeated repeated repeated or distressed flashback flash-BACK flash(back) what about sleeping more days than not do you feel disinterested in life or interested are you interested in life in living is life interested in you do you feel controlled by have you lost control over sex behavior tell me about your behavior is it your escape what is your escape when can you escape tell me tell me are you in crisis tell me tell me please look in the mirror what do you see do you see how do you feel do you feel worry feel ugly on a scale of one to ten rate your ugly ugly ugly ugly ugly ugly ugly ugly sounds like a seven that is good I've seen worse you are not the worst you are the worst ugly ugly ugly oh now it is a ten do you feel uncomfortable this is a safe space a safe space a space that is safe for you to feel do you worry tell me tell me tell me

Miss? Hello? Miss? Did you finish the questionnaire? Did you finish?

tellmetellmetellme

"What? Yes, sorry. I'm done."

Good. This was good. We're taking the first steps here. I would like to tell you the results so that we are on the same page with your treatment plan.

An apparent:
body dysmorphic   disorder
eating   disorder
depressive   disorder
post-traumatic stress   disorder

This is good. This is good. Well, I will see you next week.

I texted Mary after leaving the clinic:

He fucking said "this is good" one too many times

bitch just go back next week and do ur homework

I went home and opened a leather-bound notebook, beginning Dr. Brown's homework assignment: *Write about a place where you feel safe*. My response was a bit unconventional:

> I like watching apartment tours on YouTube of people living in small spaces—studios, tiny homes, small one-bedrooms. I enjoy watching others in their own crafted sanctuaries, in their own places of solitude. It makes me feel a little less lonely. It makes me feel attached to some sort of odd community because I'm doing the same. I perform little rituals in my space, listening to NPR's *All Things Considered* in the afternoons, playing records, doing dishes. I feel calm. Listening to public radio in my space makes me feel connected to another voice.

The next week I tell Dr. Brown all about my obsession with watching apartment tours.

Have you ever noticed that you tend to evade discussing your emotions? Choosing well-researched digressions to distract yourself instead?

His pen scribbled. He wore a sweater-vest like a substitute teacher.

In apartment tours, white hipsters show their expensive San Francisco–New York–LA–Portland–Boston studios and one-bedrooms with their abundance of plants, IKEA and V I N T A G E blended furniture, vaulted ceilings with original wood floors and fixtures circa 1920 while their corgis run around in the background and their record players coo with the sound of The Weepies or TV on the Radio or The Black Keys or The National (or Stevie Wonder for an ethnic edge). They are designers or freelance writers or record-store owners or all three at once, and the tagline reads "SEE MY $2000 SPACE."

I fucking love apartment tours. During a period of un- or under-employment two years ago, I spent a lot of time watching them for inspiration on how to decorate my first apartment, a 400-square-foot slumlord studio that was falling apart. I paid $400 a month and could barely make rent, thanks to a series of mental illnesses.

It was a lonely home; loneliness lined the walls and took up space on the sofa. My loneliness was smart and conniving. She was my least favorite Mean Girl. On days where I was stuck inside, I found fleeting contentment reading a new book or cooking veggie omelets with Tapatío sauce. But my loneliness was a shape-shifter.

In every apartment tour, the video begins with a shot of a door opening and a

"Hi! Welcome to my apartment!"

It's a cheeky allusion to *MTV Cribs*, which is infamous for a scene of Mariah Carey playing in her tub naked, surrounded by soap bubbles and rose petals. The show famously coined the phrase "This is where the magic happens," uttered before a celebrity's bedroom door opens dramatically to a view of their plush king-size bed.

My parents indulge in a similar pastime, marathoning episodes of *House Hunters*. We watch rich white people choose among three homes in the suburbs of Atlanta–Boston–Chicago–New Orleans–Houston–Phoenix. There is usually an argument over granite countertops and crown molding and backsplashes and exposed brick and white cabinets and rainfall showerheads and two and a half acres of land and midcentury modern or bungalow exteriors. My parents fucking love *House Hunters*. They might secretly be well-to-do white people. The adults on the show are likely not crude enough to speak the phrase "This is where the magic happens." In fact, we don't get to see their decorated space until the end of the episode. The lead-up to the decision often feels like a game show. The new homeowners then proceed to show off their sanctuary with pride.

I wished I had a space that I'd carved out of a hole in the earth. I'd recently moved from my tiny studio to another tiny studio in a city where I knew no one besides Mary. I visited museums and art studios like they were sanctuaries, imagining the sound of church bells as I toured them. They were the only religion I had.

In college, I learned about Tracey Emin's *My Bed* in an art history class. For much of my life, my bed had been both a refuge and a prison—it signaled safety from a judgmental world but kept me trapped with my anxieties. Emin created *Everyone I Have Ever Slept With 1963–1995* in 1995 and then *My Bed* in 1998. Her artwork generated considerable media attention over the fact that the bedsheets were stained with bodily secretions and the floor had items from the artist's real bedroom, such as condoms, underwear with menstrual blood stains, and everyday objects, including a pair of slippers. The bed was presented in the same state Emin claimed it had been in after she'd suffered there for several days. At the time, she was in a distressing suicidal depression.

27

My Bed was bought by Charles Saatchi for £150,000. The Saatchi Gallery displayed it as part of their first exhibition when they opened their new space at County Hall, London. Saatchi also installed the bed in a dedicated room in his own home. When it was later auctioned by Christie's, the piece sold for a little over £2.5 million.

So just to be clear, this diatribe you're relaying to me, you also shared it with a date you had this week? How did that go?

Diatribe?

Okay, Sweater-Vest.

I was on my second date with Zak, a software engineer who worked at a local start-up that hoped to create the next Google Maps. On our first date, I asked him the obvious question: "Wouldn't you just use Google Maps?"

"You don't understand." He shook his head, probably wondering why he decided to go out with an artist.

Everything was going well. I usually dumped most people before the second date, but he had beautiful eyes and a strong presence, and his company prevented me from ruminating on my *apparent disorders*.

Later that night we lay naked, huddled together as if there was a blizzard outside. It was August in Ohio.

Our disagreement over Google Maps reminded me of my recent Reddit argument with SkyWalker69, who cited the *Oxford* definition of racism in an argument against affirmative action. I hoped I wasn't in bed with SkyWalker69.

"This is where the magic happens," I said to Zak on our first date, after giving him a tour of my apartment with its ten-foot living area and miniature kitchen. I gestured toward the twin-size bed with a crusty old mattress and an IKEA frame I had picked from a yard sale. I could cast a spell with ease.

Later we watched an episode of *BoJack Horseman*, the one where all the animals repeat "Thoughts and prayers, thoughts and prayers," like people do when someone dies. I laughed, choking on my chamomile tea.

"Let's play twenty questions." I squeezed his muscular arm, thinking he could probably punch SkyWalker69 if I ever needed him to. I played this game with most new boys I met.

"Who was your first kiss?" he asked.

"Anthony Johnson, freshman year of high school. I missed his mouth on the way to fifth period. But we tried again. Who was yours?"

"Rebecca Harrison. She was on the cheerleading team and a pageant queen. But she started doing molly in the girls' bathroom during lunch." I imagined her waving away her college ambitions. Hands cupped like a princess.

He pulled up Rebecca's Instagram profile on his phone. Her spray tan was just the right shade of orange. She was a cross between a pinup girl and a high-fashion model. No one had to tell me that she was the American definition of beauty.

I looked down at my stomach, then my thighs. Everything was softer now. I squeezed my thighs together, hoping to conjure the smooth water balloons of my childhood, but they formed a potholed pattern. I grabbed my phone and waited for him to fall asleep so I could look up cellulite creams in peace.

Isn't it weird how everyone goes to sleep at night?

Freda Epum, *Underexpose Me*, 2015.
Image courtesy of Sol Kim.

I see. Have you considered that your comparisons to other women are unfair? Do you know that these men value their beauty more than yours? Might you be jumping to conclusions as we discussed in our session? When did these body-image issues start?

"It all began . . ." I say, emulating the tone of Bob Barker from *The Price Is Right*.

With a girl who wasn't picked for the kickball team, who launched a bright red ball into the hands of an unsuspecting twelve-year-old. "You're out!" he called. His name was Greg, and she hated Gregs. He reigned supreme over the concrete lot, the epicenter of all middle school traumas waiting to be revealed on the chaise lounge in Dr. Brown's office fifteen years later, *hmm*s and *I see*s choiring in the air.

I will take your quip about the "hmms" as a compliment. So you would say that it started in childhood? Take me there.

Hopscotch, red light green light, hide-and-seek, freeze tag, ring-around-the-rosy, kickball. She remembered explaining the rules of these games to her friend, an international student from China.

In third grade, she learned the basics of the recorder and violin and bonded with a girl named Rosie. They played freeze tag at school until one day she was frozen by Rosie and no one dared unfreeze her.

"We just felt sorry for you. You didn't have any friends," a group of girls later told her, inviting her into their inner circle of walking scrunchies. They hissed in unison.

Another girl, wearing Polly Pocket light-up sneakers, repeated this.

"We just felt sorry for you. You didn't have any friends."

Without being unfrozen, the girl ditched freeze tag, slid down the looping tunnel slide, and ran away in tears.

She was ready for lunch: a mystery-meat burger, two corn dogs, and a basket of soggy french fries.

Binge eating after stressful events became her modus operandi. Mystery-meat burgers fed her dreams of becoming a robot body devoid of emotions.

In middle school she was asked "Did you finish?" after eating a carb-heavy bowl of rice and peanut sauce. One would think she would have developed more agency as a teenager with all the bursting body hair, odor, and breasts to prove it.

In high school the idea of ridding herself of emotions acquired more urgency. Stoically she joined the track team and ran on her own for two and a half hours, morning and night. A hundred crunches in the bathroom during lunch. She fit into a tight lace dress for prom with her football-player boyfriend. High school was the primary setting for the premiere of *The Gloomy Girl Variety Show*, a serial soap opera with no sign of cancellation in sight. *The Young and the Restless* of its time. Twenty-four seasons strong.

Every night she lay awake in bed. Too afraid of nightmares to sleep, hoping to one day find sanctuary in her own body, in her own mind.

She thought to herself: Isn't it weird how everyone goes to sleep at night?

Freda Epum, *Underexpose Me*, 2015.
Image courtesy of Sol Kim.

We've talked about nightmares a few times. You've been prescribed Prazosin, right? For your PTSD?

"Yes."

Hopefully that will kick in soon. You're still seeing Zak, yes? Since you have trouble sleeping alone, have you been able to sleep next to him?

Saturday night was my third date with Zak. I checked my phone and there was a text from Mary:

hope u get sum! release the light!

So far, sex with Zak had been all right. Fine. Sufficient. He was rather focused on himself, as most men are. When we got to his house, he globbed his lips down on mine. I wiped away his drool and smirked from the corner of my mouth as if it was the hottest thing in the world. It wasn't. But his eyes were on fire when he looked at me, as if I really did possess the powers of a glow-in-the-dark vagina. He let out a high-pitched whimper like a porn star, kissing my neck and calling out words that rhyme with "hope u get sum." I was cold and tired. I remembered his ex Rebecca Harrison's legs, and I wanted to check the tracking number on my shipment of cellulite cream. He collapsed on top of me and let out a brash sigh.

"Did you finish?"

The sound of Zak's sweaty moans still rang in my ears, and I couldn't sleep. Besides, Mary had texted me about the BDSM performer Onya Cox, who had a real vagina tattooed with glow-in-the-dark ink. I went on a bit of a research binge.

Okay, that is fine. We'll see how your sleep improves in the next few weeks. I would like to circle back to our conversation about your eating disorder. Correct me if I'm wrong, but you said you had been diagnosed with this the last time you were in therapy, right?

At twenty-two, I was diagnosed with an eating disorder characterized by binge eating and starving. I thought, *This can't be right.* I wasn't impossibly skinny like the poster girls you see for eating-disorder recovery, their ribs pushing through flesh like hands from a jail cell. Another therapist asked me how long I'd been "practicing" these habits, as if I'd been fine-tuning the art of shushing my stomach. My stomach and I were the best of frenemies. I learned how to cleanse it the way a baby learns to crawl, stumbling as it goes. Some days were better than others. I thought back to my mother's "Did you finish?" after each meal as I headed to the sink to wash my plate.

"Did you finish? Oh, good job!"

I was an emotional eater who compared my body to my sister's. She was taller and curvier, and I envied her in all the ways my mother seemed to find her more acceptable. I still remember the ice-cream trucks that circled my neighborhood before we moved to a gated community outside of Tucson when I was nine. My family was now too bougie for Bomb Pops and SpongeBob-shaped ice cream with artificial flavoring, yellow dye, and gumball eyes that chipped your teeth with each little bite.

On ice-cream truck days, I'd get two treats. On days when I

stopped by the corner store after school, I'd buy a bag of Hot Cheetos with chamoy sauce to keep up with my Mexican friends, even though the sauce tasted like artificial death. I started binge eating a few years before I became suicidal.

You were suicidal at eleven?

Yes. Keep up, Sweater-Vest.

The Hot Cheetos were spicy. Not like menopausal-woman-in-summer spicy. More full-bodied. Sexy. Oh god, is that how I thought of food as a preteen? Sexy?

Like Kyle's baggy shorts that revealed the faintest edge of Hanes underwear?

Like Peter's mustache conceived with the help of his newfound testosterone?

Like Victoria's hips as she performed ollies on her skate-board, sticking the landing in her black Vans?

Perhaps food wasn't *sexy*. The thought of Peter's stubble brushing up against my chin at night gave me goosebumps, dry mouth, sweaty palms, and tingles in the place you're only allowed to talk about during health class. My parents never signed the waiver for me to learn about pubic hair, wet dreams, and that fateful day you looked down to see red staining your skirt. I found out about STDs from my sister, who guided me toward a Google image search of genital herpes. I found out about sex from boys on the bus making predatory comments about my developing breasts, which apparently were bigger than "melons."

Should I have been surprised that a young Black girl's body parts were being compared to melons? I wasn't.

Now some days are better than others. "Did you finish?"

rings in my ears whenever I waste food. It's become a place-holder for an image of my mother filled with pride. It was what I needed to flounder through life as a young adult.

Dr. Brown's pen flutters, then begins its descent onto the page.

There is a lot to unpack here.

You mention that the food did not comfort you. In previous sessions, you've detailed a history of sexual partners with whom you lacked intimacy, but you continued to see them. Do you find yourself looking for comfort in emotionally unavailable partners, as you did with food?

"It's possible." My capitalized shouts had become lowercase mumbles. Unnerved question marks.

○ ○ ○

The following week I broke up with Zak. He took it well. He asked for a goodbye kiss, which I respectfully declined. I had on a nice shade of Fenty lipstick, Wicked Wine, and knew Rihanna would be disappointed in me if I had to wipe it away in exchange for Zak's slobber. Exhausted from being emotionally direct, I went home and finished my last pill of Prazosin and waited for sleep.

My phone dinged with a new message from Mary:

hey bitch did u finish ur journal entry 4 therapy? U told me to remind u.

> Right now, I am learning to be alone. I eat alone but feel active. I'm working, putting together ingredients. I want to be alone and productive, alone and cozy, alone and free and open.

It's weird to think that everyone goes to sleep at night. Sometimes I thought that I would pay the same price as Charles Saatchi had for Emin's *My Bed*, just for sleep. I thought about selling my bed or carrying the mattress through the streets like performance artist Emma Sulkowicz in *Carry That Weight*, a piece in which she lugged around a fifty-pound mattress to rally for her rapist's expulsion from Columbia University. Perhaps sleepwalking would be my savior. But then I'd still need a mattress to sleep on.

I carried my pillow to the living room couch, a few feet from my bed. The pillow smelled of emotionally secure, well-portioned dinners. It smelled of stable disorders. It smelled of two-thousand-dollar sanctuaries. Of Diane Rehm and safety. And light, unweighted dreams.

How to Be a Terrible No-Good
African Daughter

Make sure to keep the broth. No melons, just broth. It's Christmas and I am writing the recipe for my favorite food. My mother is cooking the melons, boiling the seeds over the stove to make egusi, a thick red-orange stew with a chunky, gritty consistency—or what I, a Terrible No-Good African Daughter with no cooking skills, mistakenly thought was "African peanut soup." What I would like to do is to produce a heartfelt story that will precede my recipe for egusi soup.

My goal here is not to be one of those cooking blogs like "Casey's Cooking Corner" (a name I made up for clunky alliteration). Casey's Cooking Corner would tell you all about my seven-year-old son and our day making my famous Casey's Chocolate Cupcakes before I get to the actual recipe. Instead, my goal is to tell you how to be a Terrible No-Good African Daughter before I get to the actual recipe.

1. Allow Toto to kill your dreams of Africa.

Never in my life did I hear the song "Africa" by Toto until I moved to Ohio. After that, I heard it more times than I could count. Once when I was at a small Midwestern dive bar, the song played in the background as a friend of mine, knowing that my parents were Nigerian immigrants, asked me how I felt about it. Since I hadn't heard the song much until then, I had never paid close attention to the lyrics, the references to drums, rain, and wild dogs.

At first I wasn't sure what she was getting at by asking me what I thought of it. *Was the song's goal to capitalize on the mythical nature of Africa?* I wondered. Perhaps I'd bought into the whole thing, joining my white friends in humming the tune. When I hear the song on the radio today, I can't help but think of that conversation, one that pretty much sparked my latest identity crisis.

2. Allow your killed dreams to manifest in a need for approval by potential Toto fans.

During one of my literature classes in graduate school, we read Nnedi Okorafor's *Who Fears Death*. I sit across from a friend who speed-reads the first twenty chapters in two hours. Meanwhile I've only reached chapter ten or so. I don't tell my friend that I struggle to read the names of the Nigerian characters. I go syllable by syllable, making sure to pronounce them the way my dad would in his thick accent—though it's waned after thirty years spent in the United States. I often tell people how I wish I, too, had an accent where I could call for my "bruddah" to bring up a bowl of nsala soup from downstairs.

While we discuss the book, I'm conscious of being the only person in the room with a direct connection to an African heritage. My white classmates stumble over names like Okeke and Binta, Mwita and Onyesonwu. Mwita is also always a struggle for me. I trip between the *m* and *w*. After a few attempts, I realize that the *m* makes an "mmm" sound and the *wi* reads as "we." "Mmm-we-tah," I say, slow and steady.

My name is pronounced "Free-duh Ay-poom." For my entire life I have pronounced my last name as "Eee-pum." It was what I was instructed to do as a kid. My dad would answer to "Ay-poom" in our house, but "Eee-pum" in public. The public perception of my identity became the norm to the point where outside it just felt more natural to me to go by "Eee-pum." It was easier for non-Africans to say, and since they were the ones I interacted with on a daily basis, that's how it was. I never questioned it. I never felt any sense of whitewashing. I never felt like I was lying to myself or disrespecting my parents until I heard actress Uzo Aduba speak about her mother and the pronunciation of her name in an interview:

> I went home and asked my mother if I could be called Zoe. I remember she was cooking, and in her Nigerian accent she said, "Why?" I said, "Nobody can pronounce it." Without missing a beat, she said, "If they can learn to say Tchaikovsky and Michelangelo and Dostoyevsky, they can learn to say Uzoamaka."[1]

Having studied Michelangelo, I knew that I did not want to be a Zoe or an Eee-pum. At an awards ceremony, the announcer called my name and actually pronounced it *correctly*, but my friends noted the difference, saying it was pronounced *incorrectly*. I hadn't even told my closest friends how to properly say my name. Perhaps that was how much I was unconsciously ashamed of my culture. My curly-haired other half would kiss my hand and call me "Free-duh Ay-poom," earnestly knowing how much it meant to me. Still, when I leave messages on the phone, the Eee-pum escapes like a Freudian slip. I bet you know how to pronounce Freud.

1. Uzoamaka Aduba, "The Eyes Have It," interview by Jonathan Soroff, *The Improper Bostonian*, May 23, 2014, https://www.improper.com/arts-culture/the-eyes-have-it.

3. Add in a few pleasant adolescent memories based on interactions with the children of Toto fans.

I flash back to high school and middle school, where boys and girls in English class study *The Iliad*, play tetherball in gym class, and eat personal pizzas. Then I hear it loud and clear: *CLICK*. The Xhosa language of the Bantu people in South Africa is oh-so-very-humorously adapted by sweaty seventh graders as a follow-up greeting after I tell them my parents are from Nigeria. The *CLICK* sound of the Xhosa language is made to represent all Africans in America. If a sweaty seventh-grade boy happened to be a bit more worldly, he'd ask me if I "speak Nigerian." No, I do not "speak Nigerian," TJ, because in Nigeria alone there are over a hundred languages given the diversity of each tribe. No, I do not speak the language of my parents, grandparents, or great-grandparents. It is quite possible that the Igbo language will die with me since I'll be unable to teach it to my children. I am an island with no bridge to other generations.

4. Allow your killed dreams to manifest in an Identity Crisis™. Leave with an idea for a new band name— Identity Crisis™.

Months ago, I traveled to Boston after receiving a scholarship to attend a conference on getting your book published. I spent much of the three-day conference alone, too shy to ask many questions after embarrassing myself in front of an intimidating type-A literary agent.

"I'm a nobody MFA student trying to get published. Where do I start?" I had asked.

"Your first mistake is describing yourself as a nobody."

As she made this remark, adding that putting oneself down was something women do, her biting confidence stung me. Just a little. She was beautiful. A self-assured Black woman whom I wanted to stand closer to. I could smell her expensive perfume that I hoped to purchase at the nearest #blackgirlmagic store so a little bit of that magic would rub off on me. I would soon discover that this trip revealed more than my lack of publishing knowledge. It revealed a larger lack within myself. A lack of Blackness. A lack of Africanness. A lack of proximity to community.

I started reading about the late Kenyan author Binyavanga Wainaina. His piece "How to Write about Africa" is a satirical examination of the way the continent is often shrunk down to a country filled with tropes and empty of "taboo subjects: ordinary domestic scenes, love between Africans (unless a death is involved), references to African writers or intellectuals."[2] *A critique that could only be written by "a real African,"* I thought to myself.

2. Binyavanga Wainaina, "How to Write about Africa," *Granta* (May 2, 2019), https://granta.com/how-to-write-about-africa. Originally published in *Granta* 92 (Winter 2005).

My entire life I've been plagued by the questions of what makes a Real African™ and how I can become one. I found myself relating to other first-generation immigrants, often not of African descent. There weren't many families that spoke with the recognizable Igbo accent of my parents while I was growing up in Arizona. By the time I was twenty-five, I had no friends with whom I could share my life experiences without having to explain nearly every aspect of myself. I felt different from my friends who were Korean American, Japanese American, Taiwanese American, Mexican American, and Palestinian American, all of whom seemed to have deep ties to their places of origin through language, food, living relatives, or community. I had none of these things. I could not speak Igbo, I could not cook Nigerian food—not fufu, jollof rice, egusi, nsala, puff-puff. I had no living grandparents to connect me to another generation, I did not grow up around other Nigerians or other Africans, I had never walked the same land my parents walked for the first twenty-two years of their lives. When I meet people, I often say, "My parents are from Nigeria." It took the insistence of a stranger for me to say: "I am Nigerian." Maybe it's because when I hear these words that declare my Naija pride, I also hear another set of words: *I could not, I had none, I am not.*

After all, wasn't I just like the people that Wainaina was critiquing? "Always use the word 'Africa' or 'Darkness' or 'Safari' in your title."[3] How could I ever write about Africa when I couldn't possibly be a *real* African? Was I still the same little girl who'd play in her dad's wicker hat, pretending to be on a safari, because that's all she knew of Africa?

3. Wainaina, "How to Write about Africa."

5. Thank Toto for allowing you to wax lyrical about your Mark Zuckerberg–inspired relationship.

I thought of how different my racial upbringing has been from that of my parents. I thought of my dad, who told me that the first white man he ever saw was a Christian missionary when he was six years old. Yet here I was fucking what *Black Panther*'s Shuri would call a colonizer. And yeah, love is love and all that crap they tell you in the West, but I couldn't stop wondering what it would be like if I brought Matthew, my avid jort-wearing, *Pokémon Go*–enthusiast, Mark-Zuckerberg-look-alike boyfriend to the motherland.

A future mini Zuckerberg-Epum's fourth-grade family tree project would have to begin with Tinder. And though a mini version of us was not yet a blip on the radar, we were making plans to deepen our commitment by moving in together. I'm an obsessive media consumer, and it just so happened that our planning coincided with my binge-watching of the Netflix show *Tuca & Bertie*, which is about two anthropomorphic thirtysomething bird BFFs going through life together. Bertie had just moved in with her boyfriend and was having a bit of a crisis. She was coming to terms with the notion that she was settling down. And so, as I watched this talking songbird struggle with the idea of marrying Steven Yeun, I was forced to come to terms with the realities of my own interracial relationship.

Blended families, like all families, are beautiful, but I struggled with the idea that my children might experience their own turmoil over their "lack." I struggled with the idea that I'd feel as though *I* was the one who erased Nigerian culture from my own lineage. Little Zuckerberg would be gaining a life filled with goetta breakfasts and Midwestern manners, but would they feel the same *I am not* that I felt? If my siblings and I all ended up with white partners, what would that say about us? Is there any real point in trying to place blame in the situation? Shouldn't I just be with the person who makes me happiest? But then again, even Bertie only dates other birds.

I had a friend who also indulged in colonizer-fucking. (Sometimes humor helps.) She was about to marry her white fiancé, an adorable nerd like my Mr. Zuckerberg. Interracial dating had always been a strange occurrence for me. Somehow I ended up dating white people from the least diverse states in the US. While on a trip to Philadelphia, walking hand in hand with a white boy from Iowa, I walked past a group of Black men who broke into applause. Were they clapping for him? A very masculine congratulations on getting with a "pretty Black girl"? Or was their applause for me? For assimilating to whiteness (*in bed*, I joke in my head)? Was it for us both, for the possibility of producing a mixed-race child? It wasn't the first time I had heard the narrative that mixed-race women were better—"good hair," "light-bright," "redbone." Rappers sang about their conquests of mixed-race women. I think back to my friend and her relationship. She, too, was holding hands with a white boy when a man walked up to her and said, "You will ruin your family."

As I get older, I'm thinking more about babies. There are fucking babies everywhere now. My uterus is about ready to jump out of my skin and pop out a slimy little freeloader while I walk down the street. Is it true that my friend and I would be ruining our families? Unraveling our deep roots to the homeland of our parents? To the ephemeral home of myself?

Mr. Zuckerberg and I were getting serious. It had been months since we said the big "I love you." Him, apparently one night when I was sleeping. Me, during an argument about the prospect of me moving away after finishing my graduate degree. And now we planned to get an apartment together in Cincinnati. I was used to difference in my relationships. Him, a German, Scotch-Irish American (read: white). A nerdy small-town boy from Kentucky with dreams of becoming a rich and famous writer. Me, a Nigerian American from Arizona who'd already left home by seventeen.

During one late night drunk with nose kisses, uninhibited burp contests, and flirty smiles, I asked him if he would come with me to Nigeria for a year. It had become part of my five-year plan to spend a year in Nigeria, hopefully on a Fulbright scholarship to work on my next book project about a girl's trip home for the first time. To my surprise, he said yes, giving a sharp nod that pushed his full head of curls forward. Our love was some pretty good crap.

When I talked to my mom on the phone about my plans of going to Lagos, and possibly to the villages where she and my dad grew up, she sounded anxious. Her tone of voice was one of perpetual worry. Whether I had graduated from college or gotten my first job, always a hint of unease. "Why would you go back if you don't know anyone there?" That stung, more than a little. I resented my parents, grateful for their sacrifice but bitter about what I'd been deprived of: a sense of self. I asked her, "How would you feel if you knew nothing about the place your parents were from? If you always felt disconnected wherever you went?" She was quiet for a beat. "I don't know." Though it felt fruitless to try to explain what I knew she would never understand, her concern-tinged voice still comforted me as I lay in my bed two thousand miles away from the only home I had known, six thousand miles away from the home I had never known.

6. Cook your recipe for delicious egusi soup with the intensity of a thousand Arizona summers. Somehow email Toto the recipe so they too can be Terrible No-Good African Daughters.

But what was I even hoping to find there? Was I like every other Black American that claimed a desire to go to "the motherland," the ever-expansive land that was taken from them? I joke with Mr. Zuckerberg that it's his job to grab the umbrella during our trip to the beach because I'm too lazy to do so and it's my reparations. The joke lands, and we both laugh at the taboo. We gloss over the fact that my family would be unlikely to receive reparations because we haven't endured generational racism by way of the Transatlantic Slave Trade. A Black American friend's teasing over my lack of *real* Blackness (the kind attached to the Transatlantic Slave Trade) rings in my ear. I remember Wainaina's words: "Readers will be put off if you don't mention the light in Africa. And sunsets, the African sunset is a must."[4] Oh, how I wished to see an African sunset just like the Arizona sunsets I watched growing up. Blending maroon with red, hot orange with pale pinks.

Maybe that would be the only place I felt real,
under the African sun.

4. Wainaina, "How to Write about Africa."

Egusi Recipe

Ingredients: egusi (melon seeds) from the African market; bell peppers; chicken broth; canned diced tomatoes; onions; habanero peppers; beef (cut into small portions); chicken thigh; salsa; spinach

Directions: cook and add the sweat of one Terrible No-Good African Daughter while listening to the musical sensations of Toto.

Segment on the inner workings
of a first-generation girl

It's clear to me that my number of #SelfCareSundays will not absolve me from the capitalist machine that punishes the disabled for not becoming "just another worker." It is difficult for me to meld these two disparate ideas: labor and rest. Where do I fit? Capable of enough labor (with a whole lot of luck) to yield me steady employment and a livable wage, yet ill enough to make labor and rest a nonnegotiable marriage. This looks like writing emails in bed, writing lesson plans in bed, writing this page in bed. My permanent place of residence is Bed, USA. In grad school, a friend of mine noticed the amount of medication on my nightstand. "Are you okay?" he asked. From another friend: "Damn." "I am disabled," I tell them. "This is my reality."

This morning I am in my apartment, not the tiny studio apartment but the much larger one-bedroom in Ohio. As sublessee, I am just a placeholder here, splaying out and living until the original occupant returns. I feel as though I have arrived. As though maybe I am now what they call a responsible adult. I question if this is what I will ever be. Here on this love seat (chocolate-brown plush material with a stain I hope is unrecognizable), I am reminded of a conversation I had with Madison, a fellow Southwesterner friend I met in graduate school, about my plan to apply for a Fulbright to do research in Nigeria. I am writing about my family and acknowledging the gap in understanding that will always exist for me, the questioning I will forever engage in while trying to discover who I might have been in Jos or Lagos or Nsukka, if my father would no longer giggle when I pronounce common words or phrases incorrectly (though, let's be honest, he never giggles, he roars). I decide that a nine-month stay in Nigeria is what will connect me to another version of myself. I get lost in browser tabs on the matter.

Suddenly, lightbulb shit goes off in my head. Not the good kind of lightbulb shit where you have an awe-inspiring idea you seek to tell the world, or your best friend, or your boyfriend, or really anyone who will listen. I'm talking about the lightbulb shit where you are reminded of your conditions, your limitations, the circumstances you constantly have to consider though you forget that they're a part of you because most don't need to contemplate such matters, but you are not most. Later, while doing research on mental health in Nigeria in preparation for a possible long-term stay, I find that in Nigeria, primary healthcare workers often do not have adequate knowledge of mental-health disorders. In addition, there are virtually no mental-health services at many primary healthcare facilities.

My heart sinks and I scramble for ideas like, *Maybe I'll just get an advance on my medication?* For nine months? Unlikely. *Maybe I'll find a doctor or a therapist in Lagos?* From this information, it is unlikely. *Maybe I'll taper off. I'll be fine.* Unlikely. I think of synonyms for unlikely: rare, out of the ordinary, unheard of, inconceivable. I think of how my body is inconceivable. Of how my Western brain and all its imbalances are seemingly absurd, conjured through superstitious beliefs, like the Nollywood movies where the main character throws boiling water on witches to curse them away from the general population. I think of how I don't belong there. How I am a no-place, a no-where.

Freda Epum, *Diary of a Wet Cloud Series*, 2015.
Image courtesy of Sol Kim.

Scary Movies and Love Stories

I. Spring 2015: My blossoms shrivel.

Let us set the scene. The house is quiet, a quiet with no other suitable description than broken. Family members walk past, slow and sullen, heads tilted to avoid a painstaking view of a loved one you could just never seem to love right. The silence is so loud, so odd, that it appears to make a rousing entrance each time an awkward interaction occurs. I'll tell you right now, you'll never know booming sound until you encounter the yelling of a Nollywood movie. Core tropes: cheating and evil spirits.

The key to this household is the way sound indicates performance—the way it gestures toward emptiness and pain for our nameless heroine. The scene goes something like this: background television populated by *Judge Judy*, *Family Feud*, or *The Maury Show*; a tall dad enthusiastically shouting back at the screen; a small mom, attentive yet always heartbreakingly preoccupied by her own clouded mind; a tall brother engrossed with the booms and pows of video games; an even taller brother seen twice per year for the last ten years; a sister with a hint of spring in her earthy brown eyes, a charmer of all who meet her. Our nameless heroine is a bit jealous.

On Fridays, inside their tan-colored house, you'll find *Shark Tank* playing on the TV. Tall Dad is glued to the screen, and Tall Brother is immersed in another screen. Small Mom sleeps. Tallest Brother and Tall Sister are living hundreds of miles away. Nameless Heroine reads or writes quietly in her room, afraid to come out. On weekends, the home appears gray despite her shimmering, brightly colored fantasies of what a not-so-nameless version of herself would be doing on a Saturday night. As she lies in bed, she stares at the popcorn-textured ceiling and counts its bumps, just shy of obsessively twirling the kinks and coils that adorn her head. She needs that ceiling. It keeps her grounded amid the wavering hallucinations she experiences in her small bedroom. She barely leaves to pee or eat. The isolation allows her mind to wander, and her mind is anything but healthy.

Tucson, Arizona, is Nameless Heroine's hometown. It is a down-to-earth version of Phoenix, a place with more palm trees and better parties.

She is a plain brown girl, or so some like to think. Her eyes are so dark you can see your reflection in them. Her curvy lips measure about an inch in width. She lives in a quiet neighborhood with mostly white and Latinx neighbors, where the houses are all the same pink or tan adobe color and the homeowners' association won't let you have a tree too big. It is where she learned how to skateboard, where she broke up with her first group of friends after they forgot to invite her to play. She hates it here because it is too far from everything; she can't drive, having crashed her car two summers ago.

She is broke. She recently got a bachelor's degree but has severe depression and anxiety as well as some other stuff. In her family's Nigerian language, there is no translation for her mental disorders. Simply put, her spirit is not well and her heart is not at rest.

This brown girl is quiet, nervous, intellectual, and creative. She worries about monsters, her weight, and the blemishes on her face that her mother never fails to point out. She has slim ankles and big flat feet. She wets her kinks and coils on a regular basis because otherwise they won't curl right. She does not straighten her hair anymore and prefers it this way, medium length and parted to the side. She smells like body odor, Speed Stick deodorant, and perfume. She wears brown oxford shoes she bought for ten bucks and a sunflower dress that flares when she walks.

She gets many compliments. Some might think she's sweet and plain as vanilla ice cream, but she likes to imagine herself as a brownie sundae with your favorite topping. She washes with African black soap and softens her skin with oil. At night, she puts on a satin bonnet that makes her feel like both an old woman and a princess. She sleeps on her stomach or her side, never on her back. She drinks, smokes, and swears. She went to a women's college in New England and is tired of everyone asking her when she moved to Tucson.

Freda Epum, *Untitled Self Portrait #1*, 2008.
Image courtesy of Freda Epum.

Nameless Heroine hears Nigerian radio playing constantly in the background, the bubbling of stew in the kitchen, and smells the warm spicy aroma that only an American-born Igbo back from a predominately white institution can appreciate. There's the sound of shooting from a video game or two, and multiple televisions and computers running. At night the light humming of the electronics dies down, the music fades, and the stove is shut off.

II. Summer 2015: Quench my thirst, fulfill my desire.

Every month she looks between her thighs to peer at the thick mucus-like blood that has come out of her body. For some time, she's hoped she would bleed to death and this would be the end of her days. She'd be smarter to pray for no pregnancy each month rather than death. Sometimes she sticks her hand beneath the flow and her blood-stained fingers remind her of her wish to die, but she's also reminded of a working life cycle. She sighs in discomfort as the cramps begin.

III. Fall 2015: Scare me, institutionalize me.

In a few moments, our Nameless Heroine will be confronted by the villain of the story. One of her hallucinations is an earth-shattering monster, seven feet tall and weighing in at three hundred pounds. It is black and blue all over with hints of gray on its head. The monster is not angry, happy, or sad. The blankness of its face frightens her because it's like her own. The monster is accompanied by a plush gray cloud, raindrops flowing from it like a storm in heat. The storm floods the ground, the water looks as deep as a dark sinking tunnel. She can see her reflection in the puddle, disfigured.

The cloud and the monster hold hands. They're a loving pair that cannot survive without each other. Together, they are the embodiment of the anguish she bathes in day after day. She is delighted to make their acquaintance, to finally meet the herald figures that hide underneath the night. The three of them shake hands before bursting into laughter.

That night, the monster opens the door without knocking. Nameless Heroine is shaking, wondering if she'd locked it. She lies there wide-eyed in the dark room. Is it her imagination that eyes are looking at her? She convinces herself the monster is sleepwalking, probably for the best.

The monster disappears into the darkness, but the incapacitating fear, the paranoia, lingers. The fear is a shadowy figure that she cannot describe. It moves quickly. Only through the crack in the door can she see it. It is a nonbeing, a human morphed into a shifting collection of shadows, a soundsuit of evil. Has she seen a ghost? The Grim Reaper? She's unsure about what has taken place, but she knows it's something she never wants to see again.

All she hears are explosions. The monster and dark cloud are yelling at Nameless Heroine. Violent, brutal commands in her head. Indescribable screams. Familiar conversations. *You're no good. You're worthless. Stupid bitch.* They say mean things to her, she tells the doctor. They make fun of her. Taunting, laughing. They take pleasure in her fear. Why is she always afraid? She doesn't want to live this way. She doesn't want to be inhabited by monsters. They are calling her. She doesn't answer, but they leave a voicemail. Sometimes they leave multiple messages, as if trying to get a hold of someone in an emergency.

Her movements are slow, sinking in a quicksand pit of despair or struggling to walk through a tank filled with her

own tears.   (careful) . . . step . . . RESISTANCE RE-SISTANCE . . . step.

"So what do you do for fun?" nothing "How are you feeling today?" like shit, you? "What's wrong with you?" should be asking you that question "Do you need a hug?" no, go away "ARE YOU SAD?" "YOU SEEM DIFFERENT TODAY."

. . .

. . .

"ARE YOU IN A CRISIS?" "ARE YOU FEELING SUICIDAL TODAY?" "HOW WOULD YOU RATE YOUR MOOD?" "DID YOU HAVE A BOWEL MOVEMENT TODAY?"

Every sound she hears in the unit is painstakingly loud yet melds into her subconscious.

Her brain is unwell. Her brain has ill will for her. She spends the Fourth of July crying during the fireworks and celebration. Blue, red, and white. White light blinds her. Her sense of sound is enhanced. A superhuman connection to screams and whispers and songs in the night. She curls up in a ball to protect herself. There is no protection from herself. So she waits for the splitting headaches and heckling to disperse. She feels cursed waiting for the monsters to reappear.

Mother Nature cooks the best medicine, and it makes Nameless Heroine hungry as hell. Unlike big bottles with big pills and a long list of prescriptions, small bottles feel good in her hands. Small pills feel good sliding down her throat. Oh, the excitement of a new medicine regimen.

Pump 'em full of pills, make 'em feel like animals herding.

Knock, knock, knock!

"Freda, we're heading downstairs."

This is the first time she's heard her name today. A jolt runs through her body. Here is what it feels like when lightning greets a storm. When sparks pierce a wet cloud. But the moment is fleeting, and she remains nameless for the rest of the day.

IV. Winter 2015: I am melted snow turned to rain.

She hides her face behind Small Mom's back like she did when she was a child. She feels safe there, nestled against her mother, quietly wondering how many more times she will get to do this. As Small Mom speaks, one can almost imagine the tenderness in her voice as she became acquainted with her child in the delivery room: "Hi, baby, welcome to the world." At 5′4″, Small Mom is the smallest person in the family. It is a joy to encounter her eyes, her smile, but her smile becomes less frequent as the days go by. She embraces her daughter because her children are the only ones left to protect her from her own mind.

Small Mom immigrated to the United States to join Tall Dad in Arizona after months of exchanging love letters and the odd phone card–facilitated call. She got pregnant two years later with Tallest Brother. Worked two to three jobs to support four children. Small Mom is the strongest, most determined and resourceful woman Nameless Heroine's ever met. Nameless Heroine often compares her life to Small Mom's achievements. If only Small Mom could see herself in this light. If only Nameless Heroine could see herself in the same light.

After the deaths of Small Mom's mother, father, and grandmother, Nameless Heroine watches her mother slowly fade away. Small Mom is hiding somewhere, waiting to fight her own monsters. In a surprising way, Nameless Heroine has a chance to bond with Small Mom over their current state of affairs. For a while she is too downtrodden to tell Small Mom she looks pretty that day, her usual ritual. Now she makes sure to tell her every day.

Winter cracks her lips and skin; snowflakes of dead sun abound. Fogged-up mirrors, fogged-up lenses. Fogged-up senses. Winter clouds her vision with steamy heated vents and cloudy gray skies. Winter loves her dearly, but she has just broken up with Winter, who hasn't received the memo. The clouds come sauntering back, grayer, bleaker, better than ever. They call her name, but she resists.

Who is she kidding—she's never resisted! She joins Precipitation, a murky-eyed fellow, for a cup of hot cocoa. It goes cold quickly, so she sits calmly as Precipitation tells her about the clouds and why they're so hell-bent on following her. Mostly because she allows them to. *Gee, thank you, Precip.* They wait for spring, only to be met with corpse flowers and blackened roses.

V. Spring 2016: Dew drops replenish my heart.

"Hey, I'm talking to you!"

"Yes?" Nameless Heroine replies.

Few people have heard her voice so loud and clear. But as she speaks, the sound of her voice gives her raging headaches. She has never quite found her tongue. It's lost somewhere behind her full lips—the upper lip a kissable sable brown, the bottom an eraser pink.

She often wonders if people have lost their hearing. *They can't all be wearing earplugs or have ears clogged with nasty wax*, she thinks. Over time, some have learned to bring their ears close to her mouth as she speaks. They calmly ask her to repeat herself. Most are not so kind.

○ ○ ○

Nameless is without a name. A Jane Doe. She is unidentifiable unless otherwise accounted for. Without I, being, self. She is a No-Self, a psychological machine, a collection of wooden parts running under the assumption of agency. What does it mean for her to write these pages? To assemble a collection of stories, an archival description of recurrent suffering?

My I is fleeting.

I conjure new monsters so they can show you, dear reader, how to properly invade the world with tears. I needed to create a giant rain cloud so that I could tell you about the larger-than-life terrors that take up space in my mind. What does it mean to become best friends with a storm? I welcomed the downpour. I could not see where my skin ended and the water began.

Freda Epum, *Diary of a Wet Cloud Series*, 2015.
Image courtesy of Sol Kim.

HOUSE #2:

THE BOUNTIFUL BLACKNESS AS FEAR BUNGALOW

We walk up the steps to our next home tour. The realtor and I are making small talk. "Buying a house sure is the American Dream, isn't it?" I stumble over my words, losing my narrative footing. My response is a research essay, a play, a poem, a fantasy—anything but yes.

Crazy Eyes and the Walking Dead

When I moved to Ohio in 2017, I attended a therapy session where I asked what I should do if I ever needed to go to the mental hospital again. The young Black therapist said to call the police. I looked at her with a face both jaded and concerned.

"I wouldn't feel safe calling the police."

"Right, right, of course." Her nods affirmed what I knew to be a possible reality. I did not want to end up like Sandra Bland, dead at the hands of an officer. Sandra Bland, when killed by police, was said to have killed herself.

In the video footage recorded by the police dashcam during her arrest, she is pulled over for failing to signal when changing lanes. Something I see every day and have been known to do myself. Even as I write this, my anxiety is making up some scenario in which a cop car bursts through the walls and pins me down for forgetting to use my blinkers.

Once when I was with a group of white friends, we were pulled over because the driver hadn't received her new license plate. After the officer told us we were free to go, one of them said to her, "Why are you scared? You're a white girl in a Prius." It was not until later that I realized a deep-seated fear that the officer would look in the car and see someone who didn't belong.

Freda Epum, *Untitled Self Portrait #2*, 2008.
Image courtesy of Freda Epum.

After Sandra Bland's death in 2015, I wanted to know more about her story and #SayHerName, the social media campaign that aimed to shift the idea that police brutality only affected Black men. Articles circulating the internet stated that she was a middle-class woman on her way to her job; they claimed it made her more relatable. I know I related to her in a deep way. The *New York Times* reported that on her jail-booking screening form, she checked "yes" in response to the question "Have you ever been depressed?" The article continues, "On whether she had ever attempted suicide, the form noted 'yes,' in 2014, by using 'pills' because of a 'lost baby.'"[1]

Was it her history of mental illness that allowed the cop to go unconvicted? Headlines read: "Sandra Bland previously tried to commit suicide."[2]

It was all the media needed to convict her posthumously.

1. David Montgomery and Michael Wines, "Dispute Over Sandra Bland's Mental State Follows Death in a Texas Jail," *New York Times*, July 22, 2015, https://www.nytimes.com/2015/07/23/us/sandra-blands-family-says-video-sheds-no-light-on-reason-for-her-arrest.html.
2. Elahe Izadi and Abby Phillip, "Sandra Bland Previously Attempted Suicide, Jail Documents Say," *Washington Post*, July 23, 2015, https://www.washingtonpost.com/news/morning-mix/wp/2015/07/22/documents-sandra-bland-previously-attempted-suicide-felt-very-depressed-on-day-of-arrest.

In "Corpsing," Afropessimist theorist David Marriott describes the concept of social death, stating that "Black life *is* itself this deadly personation."[3] I wondered if my own mental-health paperwork would mark me as a "dead girl walking" by society. I wanted to find other walking dead girls—Black women living with mental illness. But there were few depictions of them.

The first portrayal of bipolar disorder I saw on screen was in *Degrassi: The Next Generation*, the Canadian television show famous for its gripping teen stories and Aubrey Graham, aka Drake. Craig Manning, a white lead character who deals with physical abuse at the hands of his father, later discovers that he is bipolar. The viewers see Craig do a variety of reckless things, such as go off his medication (a common issue), disappear into the streets, and beat up his stepdad. Manning never dies at the hands of the police.

But of course he wouldn't die; he's a teenager! Then I remember Tamir Rice and Diana Showman.

3. David Marriott, quoted in Paula Rabinowitz, "Masking: (A Response to David Marriott's 'Corpsing; or, The Matter of Black Life')," *Cultural Critique* 94 (Fall 2016): 66, https://doi.org/10.5749/culturalcritique.94.2016.0065.

I marathon *Orange Is the New Black*. In Season 7, Black Cindy throws Taystee under the bus when she falsely testifies that Taystee killed a guard in a prison riot. Suzanne ("Crazy Eyes"), a mentally ill character with a heart of gold, tries to put Black Cindy and Taystee back together again. However, Black Cindy, wracked with guilt, yells, "Suzanne, everything is broken and life is unfair. When are you gonna learn that?" It's the same haunting message the character Pennsatucky delivers when she asks Suzanne, "Do you really think you deserve to be here?"

Earlier in the series, Suzanne kidnapped a boy who wanted to play with her. The boy had jokingly climbed onto a windowsill and then fallen to his death. It didn't matter that she was trying to help him.

"But it was an accident," Suzanne tells her adoptive mother. "Is it fair?"

"No, it is not fair," she replies, staring into her daughter's eyes through the glass prison partition, phone in hand.

W. E. B. Du Bois's theory of double consciousness describes "a peculiar sensation . . . this sense of always looking at one's self through the eyes of others . . . an American, a Negro; two souls, two thoughts, two unreconciled strivings."[4] Suzanne, raised by white parents, sees herself not as Black but as human, echoing neoliberal declarations of "I don't see race." It is this unawareness of her race combined with her mental illness that leads her to believe there would be no punishment for playing with a child she doesn't know. But then Suzanne's double consciousness emerges. The logic of Black imprisonment and death has dawned on her.

4. W. E. B. Du Bois, *The Souls of Black Folk* (Chicago: A. C. McClurg and Co., 1903; New York: Dover Publications, 1994), 2. Citations refer to the Dover edition.

After Sandra Bland's death, I did my best to imagine her life. When she came home from work, did she have someone waiting for her? I imagined a scene of a "lost baby" who was lost to police brutality. *In this world, it must have happened to someone.* I checked Google to confirm my suspicions: "SEATTLE POLICE RELEASE AUDIO OF FATAL SHOOTING OF PREGNANT WOMAN."[5] I didn't listen.

5. Scott Greenstone, Steve Miletich, and Mike Carter, "'Get back! Get back!': Seattle Police Release Recordings of Fatal Shooting of Charleena Lyles," *Seattle Times*, June 19, 2017, updated November 16, 2017, https://www.seattletimes.com/seattle-news/law-justice/get-back-get-back-seattle-police-release-audio-of-fatal-shooting-of-charleena-lyles.

As I get older, I find myself wondering what it's like to live in a pregnant Black body. The Centers for Disease Control and Prevention estimates that 700 to 900 new mothers die in the US each year, and an additional 500,000 women experience life-threatening postpartum complications, with a disproportionate number being Black.[6] Further, Black infants are almost four times as likely as white infants to die from complications related to low birth weight caused by stress.[7] Even our children are deemed dead on arrival.

6. Emily E. Petersen et al., "Vital Signs: Pregnancy-Related Deaths, United States, 2011–2015, and Strategies for Prevention, 13 States, 2013–2017," *Morbidity and Mortality Weekly Report* 68, no. 18 (May 10, 2019), https://www.cdc.gov/mmwr/volumes/68/wr/mm6818e1. htm?s_cid=mm6818e1_w#suggestedcitation.
7. US Department of Health and Human Services, Office of Minority Health, "Infant Mortality and African Americans," https://minority-health.hhs.gov/infant-mortality-and-african-americans.

How does it feel to be Black, a woman, and "crazy," all while carrying another Black body inside you who could someday inherit your racial trauma? Which one is the true nail in the coffin that makes you perpetually othered? I have read many accounts by women who struggle with mental illness on deciding whether to have children. The issues resonate with me: Will I be able to devote enough care to my child if I'm sick? Will they, too, suffer from mental illness? However, it's Black women who most often speak about whether their children will be killed.

I have a nightmare: it is a horror movie about
crawling undead babies.

In "Everybody Dies," a clip from HBO's *Random Acts of Flyness*, Ripa the Reaper—a Black woman dressed as the Grim Reaper—shoves a group of Black children through a door marked Death.[8] She laughs maniacally after pushing them through and proclaims, "Everybody dies." In this reality, it seems that the children are being diagnosed with terminal Blackness. They never even stood a chance.

---

8. *Random Acts of Flyness*, season 1, episode 1, "What Are Your Thoughts on Raising Free Black Children?," created by Terence Nance, aired August 3, 2018, on HBO.

In theater, "corpsing" is when an actor breaks character due to some blunder or disturbance. The term supposedly originates from stage actors who are trying to play dead and then burst out laughing. Again I think of David Marriott's "Corpsing; or, The Matter of Black Life," where he writes, "Blacks must learn not to speak or perform life nor to desire this role. For the idea that Black life can be rendered as a livable life that 'matters' rather than a life lived in a state of injury or permanent nonexistence is to effectively transform it by corpsing the failed performance that Blackness is."[9]

It's possible that Ripa the Reaper could be deemed "crazy" by spectators. But she participates in the act of corpsing. Corpsing is, ironically, an act of sanity because it recognizes the futility of hanging on to Black life.

9. David Marriott, "Corpsing; or, The Matter of Black Life," *Cultural Critique* 94 (Fall 2016): 36, https://doi.org/10.5749/culturalcritique.94.2016.0032.

Something inside me hopes the young children will crawl out of the closet marked Death and Ripa the Reaper will be waiting, turning their zombie bodies into human flesh for the first time.

To understand how Black bodies are marked for death, it is useful to look at Black performances of death. As E. Patrick Johnson explains, "Black performance provides a space for Black culture to reveal itself to itself—to come to know itself, in the process of doing."[10] Like Du Bois's double-consciousness theory, these performances of death reveal how the Black body/subject is perpetually under attack. Not only has white supremacy marked the Black body for death, the Black body is often killed in real life. The Black subject must crawl like a zombie to escape their fate.

10. E. Patrick Johnson, "Black Performance Studies: Genealogies, Politics, Futures," in *The SAGE Handbook of Performance Studies*, ed. D. Soyini Madison and Judith Hamera (Thousand Oaks, CA: Sage Publications, 2006), 449.

These performances are rehearsed and delivered again and again, invoking J. L. Austin's concept of the performative utterance. As Austin defines it, "the uttering of the sentence is, or is a part of, the doing of an action, which again would not *normally* be described as, or as 'just,' saying something."[11] Eric Garner's dying words, "I can't breathe," become a performative utterance as they are uttered and re-uttered by activists that perform death at die-in protests. The phrase "I can't breathe" is no longer *just* a sentence; it is real. Black bodies—as dying subjects—are always gasping for air.

As Paula Rabinowitz states, "these dying black men's words, reverberating across the planet, rehearsed and reuttered . . . by those still living, call attention to the already damaged life, the already dead life."[12] It is the (re)performance of the dead/dying Black figure (through the sheer multitude of performance art by Black artists crawling, bleeding, lying, etc.) that signals an embodied/ephemeral archive of social death. The recordings of such performances via films, documentaries, and live footage are archival documentation of the absence of life.

11. J. L. Austin, *How to Do Things with Words*, 2nd ed. (Cambridge, MA: Harvard University Press, 1975), 5.
12. Rabinowitz, "Masking," 66.

By *r*epeating performative protests/acts, death is *r*eper-formed by the Black body. One example is performance artist Keith A. Wallace's "playing dead" demonstrations, in which a visceral discomfort arises yet is utterly ignored. In 2014 Wallace, a Philadelphia native and at the time an MFA student at the University of California, posed as a dead body in front of the "LOVE" statue in Philadelphia to invoke Michael Brown's shooting in Missouri. Brown's body was left uncovered on the street in broad daylight for hours. Covered in fake blood, bullet holes, and even police caution tape, Wallace lay down and stayed absolutely still for an hour—right in front of one of the busiest tourist attractions in the city. Tourists took photos in front of the statue, disregarding his body. Another member of the silent protest stood next to Wallace with a sign that read "CALL US BY OUR NAMES." Lee Edward Colston, one of the protesters and a Juilliard theater student, told *Philadelphia Magazine* about an older white couple who wanted to take a picture in front of the "LOVE" statue: "The older white gentleman said, 'Why do they have to shove their politics down our throats?' The woman replied, 'They're Black kids, honey. They don't have anything better to do.'"[13]

13. Victor Fiorillo, "Ferguson Protest: Tourists Pose With 'Dead' Teen at LOVE Park," *Philadelphia Magazine*, August 18, 2014, https://www.phillymag.com/news/2014/08/18/ferguson-protest-tourists-pose-dead-boy-love-park.

Keith A. Wallace, *Call Us By Our Names*, 2014.
Image courtesy of Lee Edward Colston and *Philadelphia Magazine*.

In "What White Publishers Won't Print," Zora Neale Hurston writes, "To others [it seems impossible] that a great mass of Negroes can be stirred by the pageants of Spring and Fall; the extravaganza of summer, and the majesty of winter . . . As it is now, this capacity, this evidence of high and complicated emotions, is ruled out."[14] The older white couple did not believe that Black people could be stirred by the pageants of Spring or Fall—this emotional capacity was reserved for the *real* humans. Black people had nothing better to do than die.

14. Zora Neale Hurston, "What White Publishers Won't Print," *Negro Digest* (April 1950), available online at https://pages.ucsd.edu/~b-goldfarb/cogn150s12/reading/Hurston-What-White-Publishers-Wont-Print.pdf.

Performance artist Pope.L is famous for his "crawls," physically excruciating street performances he staged in New York during the 1970s. His work called attention to the homelessness epidemic and how representations of unhoused people are often riddled with ableism. The imagined homeless person—tattered clothes, distressed appearance—does not present themself in a way that signals respectability.

Pope.L wore a tattered suit or an ironic Superman costume as he crawled along the pavement. Pedestrians either ignored or mocked him as a cameraman recorded the spectacle from a distance. In an account of one of these crawls, a Black man became upset, demanding that the performance end. Wearing a suit like Pope.L's, the man exclaimed, "I wear a suit like that to work!" and "You make me look like a jerk!"[15] To see another Black man crawling, vulnerable, on the ground felt familiar to him.

The Black man in the suit can be described as an "alien familiar," a term coined by cinematographer Arthur Jafa.[16] As Jafa describes it, the alien familiar occurs when images in cinema become less and less like a fictional film and more like real things. That is to say, our performative interpretations of life are merely life itself. Pope.L's crawl was too close for comfort for the spectator.

It's another dead Black person on the news—made strange through the imagery of bodies hanging out to dry. Strange, but not strange enough.

15. Nathan Taylor Pemberton, "Crawling Through New York City with the Artist Pope.L," *New Yorker*, November 22, 2019, https://www.newyorker.com/culture/culture-desk/crawling-through-new-york-city-with-the-artist-pope-l.
16. Arthur Jafa, "The Notion of Treatment: Black Aesthetics and Film," in *Oscar Micheaux and His Circle: African-American Filmmaking and Race Cinema of the Silent Era*, ed. Pearl Bowser, Jane Gaines, and Charles Musser (Bloomington: Indiana University Press, 2016), 18.

Pope.L, *How Much is that Nigger in the Window aka Tompkins Square Crawl*, 1991.
Image courtesy of the Estate of Pope.L and Mitchell-Innes & Nash, New York. © Pope.L.

Pope.L's crawls remind me of Frantz Fanon's words in *Black Skin, White Masks*:

> Look, a nigger, it's cold, the nigger is shivering, the nigger is shivering because he is cold, the little boy is shivering because he is afraid of the nigger, he thinks the nigger is quivering with rage, the little white boy throws himself into his mother's arms: Mama, the nigger's going to eat me up.[17]

To others, the Black person can never act as a human, "shivering because he is cold," but can only respond with rage. The little boy cowers in fear over being eaten up by a Black body in the same way that zombies in popular culture are seen as nonlive subjects that eat human flesh.

Pope.L's performances not only signal the image of "crazy," of homeless, of downtrodden. His fear, *the crawl*, also signals zombie. The Black figure, socially dead, is the perpetual zombie. Zombie theory notes the white supremacist fear of the Black body.[18] The corpse/zombie figure exists in a liminal space of live/nonlive. This assertion is proliferated by Pope.L's body of work, which addresses themes of the Black male body as a "lack." An "in-between space." Both Keith A. Wallace and Pope.L use their Black bodies marked for production and consumption to create an ephemeral space for performance that critiques such designations. The Black bystander who is offended by Pope.L's crawl is an example of the alien familiar. He sees the desperation in the act of crawling and the way the Black body, no matter how much we engage in respectability politics, is still regarded as perpetually dead.

17. Frantz Fanon, "The Fact of Blackness," in *Black Skin, White Masks*, trans. Charles Lam Markmann (New York: Grove Press, 1967; London: Pluto Press, 2008), 86.
18. Elizabeth McAlister, "Slaves, Cannibals, and Infected Hyper-Whites: The Race and Religion of Zombies," *Anthropological Quarterly* 85, no. 2 (Spring 2012), http://www.jstor.org/stable/41857250.

Die-ins are another kind of public death performance, a protest during which participants simulate death in areas with high foot traffic to grab the attention of passersby. They are a longtime staple of environmental, antiwar, and AIDS activism. Writer Nicholas D. Mirzoeff describes how activists created several ways of timing their die-ins: "A participant might count out 'I can't breathe' 11 times, as Eric Garner did. Or the die-in might be timed to last four-and-a-half minutes to symbolize the four-and-a-half hours that Michael Brown's body lay in the street."[19]

A crawling man, a group protest, a die-in are acts of resistance that situate us within a Black oppositional gaze. They haunt us like zombies do. In her essay "Slaves, Cannibals, and Infected Hyper-Whites: The Race and Religion of Zombies," Elizabeth McAlister writes: "Zombies are used in both ethnographic and film contexts to think through the conditions of embodiment, the boundaries between life and death, repression and freedom, and the racialized ways in which humans consume other humans."[20] The zombie is a monster with a body but no soul, spirit, consciousness, interiority, or identity. A human who's lost all trace of their humanity. This is our collective understanding of zombies in contemporary culture. But the zombie is bound up in white supremacist ideals too. Namely, the fear of the Black body.

19. Nicholas D. Mirzoeff, "How Ferguson and #BlackLivesMatter Taught Us Not to Look Away," *The Conversation*, August 10, 2015, https://theconversation.com/how-ferguson-and-blacklivesmatter-taught-us-not-to-look-away-45815.
20. McAlister, "Slaves, Cannibals, and Infected Hyper-Whites," 457.

Will these performances of Blackness, these performances between live/nonlive subjects, save future Sandra Blands? Multifaceted representations of Black people—the Crazy Eyes, the Rita the Reapers, the William Pope.Ls, Keith A. Wallaces, and die-in protesters—are forms of resistance. They allow us to move into a Black optimist space, treading lightly, if only to dip a toe in the water. It is my hope that these reperformances both on-screen and off-screen will shrink the archive of death.

I hope they will make the archive small enough that some-day I can stop asking,

Why would it matter if I died crazy when I was really dead the whole time?

Gallery of Aliens

In college I learned about Reginald Shepherd. He identified as a gay Black man and described a sorrowful view of himself within an unjust society caused by an obsession with white men. He called himself a monster.[1]

That summer I began an artist residency in Philadelphia. I painted a portrait of Kanye West with a palette knife and oil on paper, because why not? I made some connections between Kanye as a media figure and Reginald Shepherd. I painted Kanye with a palette knife and a stipple brush. I drew with charcoal and added some glitter, because why not. Beautiful. Sparkling like a Black man who loves himself. Oil degrades paper over time.

1. Reginald Shepherd, interview by Charles H. Rowell, in "Emerging Male Writers, Part II," special issue, *Callaloo* 21, no. 2 (Spring 1998): 290–307, https://www.jstor.org/stable/3299426.

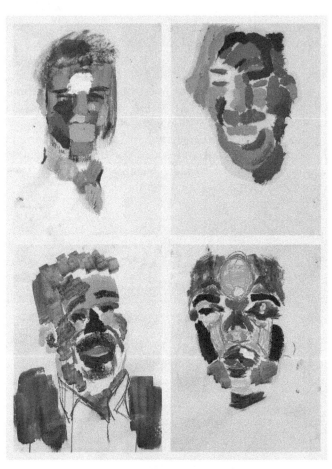

Freda Epum, *Everything My Mother Taught Me (Disintegration)*, 2014. Image courtesy of Freda Epum.

Word association from Kanye to monster to Reginald Shepherd to hate to Black bodies somehow leads me to Trayvon Martin. It's like when you're on Wikipedia and you somehow end up on the page for the Bible after searching for Matthew McConaughey. I paint Trayvon Martin's teenage face, knowing I am only eleven months and 342 days older than him. I think of the other people dead or beaten by blue people. Those who proclaim #BLUELIVESMATTER likely wouldn't be fond of being called blue people. Like the blue penis that swings around in *Watchmen*, like the Blue Man Group, like Maggie Nelson's obsession in *Bluets*, like the blue skies of heaven. No, not like the beautiful periwinkle blues. More like blue-black faces—broken. So I paint more, until I have about sixty. Sixty dead or beaten bodies. My studio becomes a morgue or a funeral or an emergency room or maybe all of them at once.

I'm not a good artist. I don't wear much black. I worry that I'm being disrespectful at the funeral in my bright red spaghetti straps and purple shorts. I make sure to write down the names of each person. How could I continue their erasure? No. Sixty names to remember. I don't know those names anymore. It's been six years since I juxtaposed crimson with ultramarine blue to depict a broken nose. Or mixed azure with burnt umber to make a color that looks black but isn't quite. When it came to presenting the paintings at the exhibition, I placed an old toolbox next to them. It had little individual compartments that resembled old mailboxes or lockboxes in bank safes. I count the compartments. Sixty. I decided to title the piece "Everything My Mother Taught Me" and "Disintegration."

We are sorry to inform you about the banana peel thrown at the Black girl: A One-Woman Show

Setting: A woman stands at center stage. The audience's seats are on a platform, allowing the performer to make direct eye contact. She is wearing a black top and a black skirt. The background shows illuminated streetlights. She begins a one-woman show, offering a series of monologues before asking the audience to participate in an interactive performance. Props litter the stage, such as a small desk with a journal, a bucket of water, a rag, a small mirror, and a bucket of white paint. A screen projection casts the color white onto her body.

TAPED VOICE OFFSTAGE:
"Stand in the evening light until you become
transparent or until you fall asleep."
—Yoko Ono, 1961[1]

I'm always a victim. And you know what? I am tired of being a goddamn victim. Am I tired of being a goddamn victim? I am tired of being a goddamn victim. So let me tell you a story. Last night I'm walking in the middle of the night. It is about midnight. I am not concerned because, you know, we live in a small town, and there's not much danger. Right. Well . . . except for the sexual assault email notifications that we receive about once a week. But that's not me. This is not a story of sexual assault.

She sits down and she's on the phone. The screen projection changes to a bright blue background that's cast on her face, then to a picture of a teenage girl's bedroom.

1. Yoko Ono, "Body Piece," in *Grapefruit: A Book of Instructions and Drawings* (Tokyo: Wunternaum Press, 1964; New York: Simon & Schuster, 2000).

Hello? Hey girl.

TAPED VOICE OFFSTAGE:
Wah wah wah wah wah wah wah wah

She looks directly into the audience. She stands up and hangs up the phone. The screen changes to a bright orange, the color opposite of her mood.

But something was taken from me. So where was I? I'm walking down Beech Street, just minding my own business, when a group of frat bros walks by. I usually avoid them. Something about white men in groups wearing boat shoes. I know some people tend to cross the street when they see a Black person, but I flip it around. I subvert the issue. I'm afraid at this moment. I'm afraid during many moments.

She contemplates. Her face is visibly sorrowful.

My brown doesn't wash off.

She looks directly into the audience, scrubbing her skin frantically. The screen projection changes back to the color white.

So, I'm walking down the street, probably because I can't sleep or I have too much energy. That week I had been feeling a bit manic. I was a bit paranoid, a bit distraught. Nothing seemed to be working. I tried Advil and Ibuprofen, Naproxen, Klonopin, whiskey, the works. Not all at the same time, of course, I wasn't looking to kill myself! At least, not that day.

But fuck, I keep getting distracted.

There's a cue card that says "Please throw these at me," placed next to a bucket of pills. The audience members begin throwing various pills at the actor. She darts across the stage trying to catch them with her mouth. She knows they're Adderall.

Thank you, that's better. *(Chugs water)*

While I'm walking, I have a bit of a saunter in my step. I've been working out at the gym and lost about ten pounds and, you know, I'm feeling good. I'm feeling real good. I finished all of my finals and I am ready for the summer and the world is waiting for me.

She's pacing while swinging her hips from side to side. She moves quickly up and down the aisles.

And then I see the car slow down.

She moves slower, bringing her feet to a halt.

Hey, nigger!

She looks blankly at the audience. An audience member throws a banana peel at her face. She is still looking blankly.

(Whispers) You know, a watermelon would have been a little bit more creative.

But that's it. I'm walking down the street at midnight and a bunch of white guys in boat shoes heckle "nigger" at me and laugh loudly, aggressively, as if that's not the end of it. Tears are streaming down my face out of anger, out of embarrassment, out of fear—tears are streaming out of tears. Endlessly. *Time feels frozen* and my saunter stops and I'm not feeling fucking good anymore; it's almost as if I gained those ten pounds back. Ten pounds of racial slurs weigh down my body and nothing will fix it. Not running, not lifting, not liposuction. Well, maybe death. But death is what I'm afraid of for once.

An image of a ship is now projected on her body. She sits down. She puts on her black plastic glasses and picks up the book Zong! *She sits down at a desk, then puts the book down, pulls out a leather-bound journal, writes, then stops to return back to the scene.*

But fuck, I keep getting distracted.

So as I think about the racial violence, I'm wondering if the next course of action is for them to hang me in the trees. The greenest trees I've ever seen. Maybe in front of King Library or near Western Campus. Oh, the daycare! Yes! Strike fear in all of the Black children. "This is what will happen to you when you're Black and alone."

> TAPED VOICE OFFSTAGE:
> Aren't we always alone?

She scrubs her skin again.

At this point, I'm not sure what to do. "What do you want?" Yeah, yeah, shout that! No, don't antagonize them, pick your battles.

They just made a fool out of me and you're telling me to pick my battles?

She steps to the side and sticks her hands up, gasping with fear.

She steps to the opposite side and gestures as if she's holding a rifle. She cocks it and then shoots into the audience.

Boom.

But that's all in another world. You really think I would shoot someone? I know you guys think I'm bad because I'm over here shaking my hips when I walk alone at midnight, but I'm not that bad!

So where was I? At this point these guys are just staring at me and I'm staring at them and it's only a few moments between here and what happens next. One of them—the biggest one—gets out of the car and starts chasing me. He has to chase me because there's no way I would have just stood there! So I'm running through the woods in this suburban-ass white-bread town and it feels like I'm in a scene of Jordan Peele's *Get Out*.

But the guy finally reaches me. At this point I am so scared. I remember a friend told me they recently saw a group of men in the next town over dressed in Ku Klux Klan hoods. I remember that a picture of a noose recently appeared on a student's social media account.

An audience member throws a sponge saturated in white paint at the protagonist's head. It splatters on her face, leaving behind traces of paint. She steps back, surprised, and then smiles. She picks up the sponge and wipes more white paint on her face to finish the job.

Yes, thank you for reminding me of what happens next. So after he's thrown a sponge at me, he runs away. I hear the sound of muscle bros laughing in the distance, yelling, "Take that, nigger." And I—

TAPED VOICE OFFSTAGE:
Don't you wish you could wash it away?

What are you talking about?

TAPED VOICE OFFSTAGE:
Wash the dirt away? Wash the skin away. Wash the brown away. Wash the pain away. Wash the difference away.

Sometimes I do, actually.

There is a sign that appears: "Wash me, please." With a bucket of yellow sponges dipped in white paint. The sign also reads "$100 compensation."

She takes off her shirt and skirt, revealing a white shirt and shorts underneath. She scrubs her skin.

Please help.

A group of audience members comes up and wipes white on her skin.

That's enough, thank you.

She steps away from the audience and wipes her face to reveal her brown skin.

TAPED VOICE OFFSTAGE:
How do I look?

How do I look?

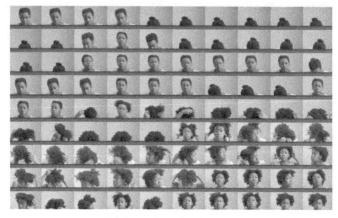

Freda Epum, *Leftovers*, 2014.
Image courtesy of Freda Epum.

I began the day thinking

After a period of writer's block, I gave myself the task of writing a poem a day. I was working on a project called "Microprocessing (The Interesting Subject)," where I set to record or document (creatively, I suppose) or write down or marvel at or ponder or wonder about a series of what the academics call microaggressions—everyday verbal and nonverbal derogatory acts or communications against a member of a marginalized group. Now I'm writing about my own experiences. I read a book by Renee Gladman called *Calamities*. She begins each poem with "I began the day thinking," giving herself the task of writing about what happened or what would happen to her each day.[1]

I began the day thinking about what would happen if I destroyed the day and wrote my own.

1. Renee Gladman, *Calamities* (Seattle: Wave Books, 2016).

Microprocessing: composition

I taught a class where I assigned my students Audre Lorde it was her essay "The Transformation of Silence into Language and Action" the essay that says "I am standing here as a Black lesbian poet, and the meaning of all that waits upon the fact that I am still alive, and might not have been."[1] And I was standing there with many of the markers Lorde has, and one student says, "She just wants us to feel sorry for her because she is Black and gay." And I didn't know what to do and there are often many moments where I don't know what to do and deep down I know that I never make the right decision and in this moment I was silent and I knew that Audre would be disappointed in me I don't know if Audre Lorde and I would be on a first name basis if I were to have met her because I was silent when I should have spoken I know this because she says and says and says "I have come to believe over and over again that what is most important to me must be spoken, made verbal and shared, even at the risk of having it bruised or misunderstood."[2] And in this moment my voice feels meek and my heart feels heavy and my head is spinning with action how dare you action do you not see me standing here in all of my brownness action whywhywhy action I see you action when will my brownness be seen as greater than difference action when will I be able to say and say and say

~~violence happens to me when~~

1. Audre Lorde, "The Transformation of Silence into Language and Action," in *Sister Outsider: Essays and Speeches* (Berkeley, CA: Crossing Press, 1984), 40. Paper delivered at the Modern Language Association's "Lesbian and Literature Panel," Chicago, Illinois, December 28, 1977. First published in *Sinister Wisdom* 6 (1978) and *The Cancer Journals* (San Francisco: Spinsters, Ink, 1980).
2. Lorde, "The Transformation of Silence into Language and Action," 40.

after the boy tells me Audre just wants us to feel sorry for
her because she is Black and gay I speak up to say say say
who is this us it is not my us it must be your us because I do
not feel a we in this declaration I do not feel a community
in this assertion I feel a singular an I that does not belong
to me and I say this all to him and my voice is no longer
meek but speaks with urgency bursting from all corners I
form a plurality with my words

Freda Epum, *Diary of a Wet Cloud Series*, 2015.
Image courtesy of Freda Epum.

Microprocessing: brunch
After "The Bridge Poem" by Donna Kate Rushin

I am sick of being the INTERESTING SUBJECT in the literature seminar on the FEMINIST DAY I am sick because I cannot explain this to my mother or my mother to my father or my father to my sister or my sister to my brother but maybe I can explain it to my niece & nephew when they are older because of course they will go to a FANCY LIBERAL ARTS SCHOOL like I did but hopefully not have the student loans that I do I am sick of being the crazy one at holiday dinners I am sick of being the odd one out at Sunday brunches I order a big stack of chocolate-chip pancakes to drown out the UNINTERESTING SUBJECTS at the local Denny's I am sick of being the sole Black friend to 34 individual white people I sit at brunch with 34 individual white people we are not at a big buffet table like on Thanksgiving where I am the crazy one but we get to sit on top of each other while the waitress is slow because she sees that there is an INTERESTING SUBJECT among the other UNINTERESTING SUBJECTS one of the UNINTERESTING SUBJECTS with the sideswept bangs tells me it's like I'm not even Black ya know? another with the 1990s bowl cut tells me I'm not like the other girls but I'm not a Mandy Moore girl-next-door type I am an INTERESTING SUBJECT that goes to class the next day we are studying Heidegger & it's like the white boys just ordered chocolate-chip pancakes hungry suddenly I become uninteresting again

~~violence happens to me when~~

during brunch when I sit with 34 individual white people I
flip tables   flip

---

flip

---

flip
chocolate chips go flying like flapjacks like alien saucers
I am very interesting alien now

Microprocessing: Heather goes to the mega mall

Every time I go in a fitting room I hate my body fitting rooms hate my big body synonyms for big

far-reaching	towering	voluminous
mountainous	monumental	full-figured
astronomical	Herculean	well-fed

fitting rooms love well-fed girls my high-definition high-shine high-bitch mirror loves my well-fed body my well-fed thighs and well-fed sags and well-fed tummy and well-fed cheeks my high-shine bitch mirror tells me what is your far-reaching butt doing in those Abercrombie jeans she tells me it's high time your astronomical ass starts running marathons this high-shine bitch let's call her Heather likes to hate my body ill-fitting body voluminous body so this body drops a full body's worth of monumental cash on the next size up to make my big body

compacttoypocket   this   high shine body   starts the

Heather diet

~~violence happens to me when~~

I try the Heather diet three times heatherheatherheather I feel like I'm in the movie *Heathers* once I played a drinking game with friends where we drank every time they said Heather I was so drunk the next day I had a beer belly turns out the Heather diet does the opposite of its intentions back at the mega mall I enter with a few six-packs and smash the bitch mirror to pieces

Microprocessing: Flu Shot

at the doctor yesterday there is a nurse gold hair like corn-flowers ohio girl she wears a badge that says Ohio Girl or in my dream I imagine her telling me oh I'm just an ohio girl in the office she gives me a flu shot there is no blood unlike the ohio pilgrims like the city of destruction so blood so much so the red blends into the arm of darkness hides itself among the flowers on my shoulder the prickles of hair on the arm of darkness there is no blood to Ohio Girl too dark for sight too dark to be a cornflower

~~violence happens to me when~~

I wade through rivers and burn down hospitals for laughs

Race Day

If it wasn't for the fact that your skin is brown, your hair is curly, your eyes are black and almond shaped, and you've got a nice ass (or so you've been told), you'd think there were no Black people in Oxford, Ohio. You count on your hand the number of conversations you have with another Black person in one week. Three if you're lucky, and one is your therapist. It's as if you are an alien with green skin, suction cups for hands, one eye, and an antenna that sticks out of your head. Like that purple Teletubby on the show you used to watch when you were little. Embedded in your chest is a surveillance video of Michael Brown's death, which you carry to plead your humanity. It's a part of you, but no one cares, and it's on to the next Teletubbies video. Nice try.

You spend weeks in Arizona wandering through the desert and taking pictures of those cute multicolored adobe houses that line the streets of downtown. You cry on New Year's when the boy you love tells you that the two of you can't be together. You call him It'll-Be-Nothing-but-Heartache-Boy. He tells you he loves you with his eyes despite this. You were once explosive. Bursting manically. But today what are you? Happy? Not quite; you cry again on New Year's. You wander through the desert past a bright cyan-colored adobe house with stop sign–red trim. There's a BLACK LIVES MATTER sign posted in the window. You wander through the desert past the you who cries over some dumb white boy, past the you who cries over a mother who never fails to belittle you seconds after you tell her you love her. "What's wrong? You don't look bright," she says. You walk past the door and go up the stairs to your parents' house and you text your friend to tell them that you hate it here and you're not sure why you've come. You hear some dumb white boy on the TV downstairs and your dad yelling "fool" and "cow" at the dumb white boy with the red face in the

White House. You think of how when a Nigerian calls some-one a cow, it's pretty much the worst insult an individual can call you. You think of the time your friend Taylor tells you about the BLACK LIVES MATTER sign her landlord told her to take down in Ohio. And then there's the sinking feeling; this is America and she hates you.

You sit in an elementary school classroom and your feet dangle off the floor. You're wearing the dope light-up sneakers your mom bought you from Payless, your melon-orange overalls, and your *Spy Kids* backpack. You're innocent and fly as fuck. You look down at the English class assignment and you find out you'll be reading Langston Hughes's "Harlem." Another alien, you think. You read stories by other dead dumb white boys (oh, and Emily Dickinson) for the rest of the year. What happens to a dream deferred? Maybe it just sags like a heavy load.

At this time you're too young to think of all the ways America hates you.

Your feet can touch the ground when you sit now but you're still innocent (and fly as fuck). Your friends at school are mostly anime-obsessed white girls and one Latina. You no longer fit into your melon-orange overalls or your dope light-up sneakers. A checkered pink knapsack sags like a heavy load on your back. All the cool kids have more expensive JanSport bags. The bell rings and all the kids run away from four square and tetherball back to class. You're running and you bump into another alien—she disappears like a phantom. You learn about Booker T. Washington and the Tuskegee Institute in Social Studies, but you don't hear the name W. E. B. Du Bois until college when light-up sneakers are a thing of the distant past. When you find out Du Bois was under surveillance by the FBI, you figure you never learned about him because he was too militant.

By now you're old enough to think of all the ways America hates you.

It's Black History Month and you have zits on your chin. You're in high school, writing variations of Mr. & Mrs. Vasquez in your notebook (and Mrs. & Mrs. Torres). You start dating a football player, another alien like you. They're serving fried chicken and watermelon in the cafeteria because, you know, Black History Month. Everyone asks you if you celebrate Kwanzaa. At this time you hate Black History Month. It reminds you of the time your Mexican friend's grandmother apologized that there was no soul food while walking out the door. You wish your alien boyfriend had been there.

You're on a college campus in Massachusetts sitting in a film class. The professor goes through the syllabus, and you're excited for the semester, especially the end, when you get to "Multiculturalism and Other Perspectives." You think of all the other class periods you've had devoted to race. One out of 180 days in the school year. You appropriately name them "Race Days." You walk past Race Day and try to go back. She's gone like a phantom, like the alien girl you bumped into after four square. She stands in the front of the bus but in a sea of dumb white boys. You've only met her a handful of times, but you think she's fly as fuck. She has a television embedded in her stomach that plays *12 Years a Slave*, only with a twist ending—Brad Pitt doesn't save the day because Solomon Northup saves himself. Race Day cries again on New Year's Eve remembering the shooting of Oscar Grant. She sheds one tear and then many, covering her body like the brightly colored cyan houses you walk past in the desert.

Soon there is an ocean of tears, a river of tears that extends from Arizona to Ohio to Massachusetts and back. The tears surround you and you nearly drown in them—you and your alien boyfriend, light-up sneakers, orange overalls, *Spy Kids* backpack, tetherball, and fried chicken. You board a bus in Ohio one day and see a sea of Black people. At the cross streets of Hamilton and Chase Avenue, there's a cool comic book and record store that catches your eye. You leave the sea of Black people and rummage through some comic books, looking to spend your last twenty dollars before your paycheck comes tomorrow. You start reading a comic about a fly-as-fuck feminist like you, you think this is the one. You flip through the pages and the blond feminist character stops saying "I am deliberate and afraid of nothing" and starts saying "nigger." You hear it over and over and over as you flip through the pages, and you wonder what the artistic merit of this is. Again, you hear it—nigger, nigger, nigger. You can't even remember what the rest of the comic is about because you're too busy thinking

this is America and she hates you.

You walk past an alien wearing a BLACK LIVES MATTER T-shirt. The bus with the sea of Black people swoops around the corner and you board. There's a bustling conversation over Langston Hughes and Booker T. Washington and W. E. B. Du Bois and Madam C. J. Walker and Josephine Baker and Ida B. Wells and you see Race Day in the corner and she's smiling. Her tears have stopped and her screen is glowing.

Freda Epum, *Untitled Self Portrait #3*, 2008.
Image courtesy of Freda Epum.

HOUSE #3:
THE IMPERFECTLY ILL
ISLAND ABODE

In *How It Feels to Be Colored Me*, Zora Neale Hurston writes: "I feel most colored when I am thrown against a sharp white background . . . I feel my race. Among the thousand white persons, I am a dark rock surged upon, and overswept, but through it all, I remain myself."[1] I notice that when I am put against a sharp white background, my mother is erased. I do not inherit a rich Igbo accent. Whiteness cannot spot my Nigerian lineage—the first way I came to know myself, in my first home with my family. The ways I have experienced my Blackness up until this point—growing up in predominantly white and Latinx cities and attending predominantly white institutions—is as an other, as hyper-alone.

1. Zora Neale Hurston, "How It Feels to Be Colored Me," in *I Love Myself When I Am Laughing . . . And Then Again When I Am Looking Mean and Impressive: A Zora Neale Hurston Reader* (New York: Feminist Press, 2020), 149. Essay originally published in *World Tomorrow* in 1928.

By the last leg of this house hunt, the realtor is familiar with my story. I became sick last—it is the most recent way I've come to know myself, a new mark on my body. Through my Blackness and through my illness, I learn the importance of safety, grow to value it more than ever before. When I feel safe, I am most distant from my existential fears of being Black and alive in America while I try to find my place in it. But my path to safety is not linear, characterized by PTSD flashbacks and episodes. I wind the corner and find another dip.

Freda Epum, *Diary of a Wet Cloud Series*, 2015.
Image courtesy of Sol Kim.

Flashback: Interviews

The first time I went to the psych ward I was twenty-one years, six months, and five days old.

I had been out of college for two months. My relationship had ended, and I'd failed to tell my then boyfriend, Bony-Shoulder Boy, that I'd been hearing the voice of a woman with disheveled hair and red lipstick, cold snake skin and a hiss in her voice. Then I also began hearing the voice of a grossly unshaven older man. The two were a lovingly dysfunctional couple. I never imagined them with a family. But perhaps I was their child, one whom they berated with *stupid, crazy bitch* and *no one wants you*.

Before we broke up after college, Bony-Shoulder Boy and I settled on Skyping every weekend. Before I moved from my college town in Massachusetts back to Tucson, we sat in his messy room in a beautiful historic house with five roommates—plus a basement dweller—and the loving cockroaches who "weren't hurting nobody." I asked him if we should end things, and he said no. I stared at him with a concerned look, the kind where you know this is the end but you're in denial so you keep things going for three more months until you finally break up after a five-minute phone call. It fills the emptiness in your mind where your one-year anniversary should be.

Bony-Shoulder Boy and I Skyped every weekend until every weekend turned into every other weekend and then, when my dad lay in Mercy Medicare Hospital, not much at all. Messages signing off with "love from 3000 miles away" and "love from the desert" became terrible sobs detailing my father's imminent surgery after a severe stroke. I never mentioned the fact that I'd seen his eyes roll back in his head and his lifeless body being dragged from the bed to the floor, where paramedics yelled "CLEAR, CLEAR" like they do on episodes of *ER*.

When my dad came to, he didn't remember what had happened. We'd argued rather explosively over whether I should work at Goodwill after graduating from Smith College, an elite women's college in New England. "Your family's so dramatic," my friend always told me. She was right.

I started drinking. Nothing fancy, just small plastic bottles of vodka from the gas station. A particularly hard day called for the large bottle of vodka, the one in the high-end plastic container with the red-and-black trim. I made sure to look intently at the prices—$4.25, $6.50, oh! $3.99. That's the one. At the time I was using the little money I earned at a vegan café appropriately named Veggie Circle. I hid all the bottles in my room out of fear my mother would find something in my underwear drawer while putting away laundry. My therapist mentioned that adult children have little autonomy as adults living with their parents. So I hid my bottles in the drawer with my old school notes, dressed in cloak-and-dagger.

My agoraphobia manifested in a fear of being in situations where escape could be difficult or where help wouldn't come if things went wrong. Agoraphobia, so I've been told, is a disorder characterized by symptoms of anxiety when a person perceives an environment to be unsafe with no easy way out.

After graduating college, during The Crying Years, I started going to both dialectical behavioral therapy and group therapy. I had muddled through an agoraphobic stupor but still felt susceptible to its clutches. On the shuttled drives from my house to group, I slurped on my carefully concealed vodka-spiked gas-station slushie in peace.

After graduating, I was a lifeless, unemployed zombie. On the way to an interview, I began sobbing in the car with my brother, a sweet guy who takes no bullshit. I learned all the tricks to succeed at interviews, all the stupid acronyms like STAR: Situation, Task, Action, Result. The Situation was an interview with a new-age health clinic for a communications associate job. The Task was to do the damn interview and get the hell out. The Action was to go into the restroom and recite carefully constructed answers to hypothetical questions I'd written down in my leather Moleskine and my Trying Too Hard & Co. manila folder trimmed with gold-foil polka dots and purchased at an upscale mall in Arizona. Too bad Trying Too Hard was never my strong suit. It resulted in panicked swings between "I would be the best candidate" and "I am the worst. I am a failure." While my former classmates were getting jobs at *National Geographic* and the Smithsonian and appearing on magazine covers, I was stuck in Tucson in a bad economy. My Indeed.com account read "296 jobs applied." In Tucson, there was no opportunity. There was no easy way out. I was not just *fearful of* being trapped; I was trapped. Agoraphobia wasn't something I had; it was something I was.

My next interview was at a fancy hotel, The District. I wore a navy blazer with no collar that my mom bought me as a graduation gift, a gray pencil skirt, and a multicolored orange button-up. "You gotta show that you're creative in your style, that you're an artist," my sister always said. I slipped my feet into simple black flats in case I needed to run.

I saw the interviewer out of the corner of my eye. She wore a sleek suit, her handshake was strong, and her eye contact was deep and long. My unconvincing handshake was a step up from limp, and I avoided eye contact like the plague.

I ran toward the back of the building and slumped to the ground, sighing in defeat. The best action would have been to cry alone, dust it off, be strong. Instead I called my ex-boyfriend and proceeded to cry for the next forty-six seconds. He swiftly hung up without a goodbye or an "Are you okay?"

"You're always sad," he used to say. He was right.

Another interview was at a large call center where nearly everyone in the city worked. I filled out a basic online job application that included a section where they asked what my ideal environment was. I selected the best answer from multiple choices. Options for a call center: "I know how to work a phone." Or: "My ideal environment is secluded away from others." You know, simple. I left the interview, again without a job in hand, and began to cry in my brother's car. He said something like "Chin up, be strong."

I went home and marched up to my room, closing the door with my chin held low, *weak* written across my chest. I lay in bed for several days, not eating, drinking, or bathing. To leave my room was to enter the battlefield, where a sniper could strike at any second. The mission was to not come face-to-face with a barrage of bullets. Curled up into a ball, my legs heavy and face blank, I'd been conquered by grossly unshaven father and snake-skinned mother. She kissed my forehead and left behind a red stain.

Branded like the crazy, stupid bitch that you are.

The snake-skinned woman and scruffy man were real to me. My job is to make them real to you. I want to create lingering hallucinations to give you a peek inside my brain.

Over the course of the next few months, this was my primary occupation: lifeless, room-bound zombie. I existed in a space that, if I was looking on the bright side, I thought of as a small studio apartment. Offers of food were met with "I'm not hungry!" Later I'd slip into the kitchen and binge whatever I could find, hoping it'd be enough to last me a few days. Gradually I got the courage to use the bathroom. Then I managed to go down the hall and watch my brother play *Grand Theft Auto*. Finally I became brave enough to go downstairs, to utter the words, "Hi. Can I have some food?"

I'm looking for a word other than "angry." Livid? Enraged? Heated? But frankly, I was just really fucking angry. I felt like a failure compared to my fellow college graduates. I was angry that I was still living with my parents. Angry that I had to attend therapy multiple days a week as a refuge from nothingness. Angry that Bony-Shoulder Boy never called and that the large plastic bottles of vodka weren't enough to make the hurt go away. Angry that I was a disappointment. Angry that I was alive. So damn angry.

Many people associate suicide with selfishness. I've always thought it was selfish to be worried about yourself when that person is in such utter despair. I have thought of suicide since I was eleven years old, possibly before that. In seventh grade I tried to drown myself. I sank down in a community pool only seven feet high, surrounded by friends who I believed would just let me die, or I hoped they would. Eleven-year-olds are pretty dumb. I didn't tell anyone else until the first time I went to the psych ward at twenty-one years, six months, and five days old. I didn't realize the pool incident was a suicide attempt. A repressed memory, they said.

The second time I tried to kill myself I was a sophomore in college. Sometime between 3 a.m. and 4 a.m. I walked downstairs to grab a new set of knives that a housemate's family had gifted to the dorm. Everything was cool, calm, slow. I walked with my head held high. Strong. I grabbed one of the knives in a firm handshake. Deep, longing eye contact. I went back upstairs to my room and stared the knife down. It was black and silver with a shiny blade I made sure to sharpen to get it just right.

The knife hovered close to my neck, making a small incision as I slid it across my skin with little force. *Idiot*, I thought. *Pathetic*. I hadn't even written a suicide note. I guess that was pretty selfish. The next few times I tried, I had a prewritten note ready.

Employee of the Month in *How* Not *to Finalize a Suicide.*

Freda Epum, *Untitled Self Portrait #4*, 2008.
Image courtesy of Freda Epum.

Soon after, I called my sister, holding back tears. She asked me if I was okay. I said yes. We talked about plans for Thanksgiving. And just like that, my interview with the knife was over, and I didn't get the job.

My parents didn't believe I was suicidal. *Oh well*, I thought. *More knives for me.*

I told all of this to the strange man in the ambulance on the way to my first psych ward. He looked at me with a blank face and I looked back, laughing internally, amused with sorrow.

When I arrived at the psych ward, I was held in a waiting room where they packed mentally ill patients together like anchovies, like bodies in underfunded sick units, like in slave ships. Everything moved faster than it should have.

I was hallucinating, but I was aware that I was hallucinating. The doctors called that omniscience. I saw a woman being restrained by employees while crying out to the gods, and I thought, *Where the hell am I?* But I checked myself in because I was afraid I would try to kill myself again.

At the Crisis Action Center (or CAC), I relinquished control as soon as I confirmed the statement "I am a danger to myself and others." I'm reminded of a conversation my dad and I had about a Yale student who killed herself with cyanide she ordered on Amazon. My dad went off about how she was a danger to others, and I spouted back statistics showing how people with mental illness are more likely to be victims of violence than perpetrate it themselves. We are nearly three times more likely to experience violence than those who don't have a mental illness.

How could a mentally ill person be capable of murder when they don't even have the energy to take a shower? I thought as I cried in the shower at the CAC, using lotion as leave-in conditioner.

It seemed they thought crazies didn't need Shea Moisture.

The wardens didn't let us use pens—makeshift weapons. But they did let us have those felt-tipped markers you would use in elementary school. They gave us composition notebooks because it got lonely being locked up on the top floor with a girl who routinely set her room on fire. Luckily CAC romance kept me company. I was crushing hard on a veteran with PTSD fourteen years my senior. He was heckling a girl who kept switching the TV from BBC News to *Keeping Up with the Kardashians*. I gazed across the room at them while I ate a ham-and-cheese sandwich from the cafeteria. The veteran had the sweetest crow's feet.

I became friends with a musician, Andrew, and an OCD patient, Meredith. We saved all the pudding cups and fruit snacks, claiming we never got ours during med pass, when they fattened us up to increase the effectiveness of the medicine. Med pass was a wonderful early-morning and late-night ritual where we assembled like we were waiting in line for a Juicy J concert, eager for our lithium like it was a backstage pass. My meds included Effexor and Ativan and Trazodone and Geodon and Topamax. The "ands" were endless.

In the hospital I hoped the veteran's leg would shift a little, graze my skin. In song with each other. He brushed his leg against mine through our hospital scrubs. I squirmed in my chair and held back a smile. Our eyes met the way two old friends passed each other in the hallway. They lingered.

For the rest of our stay I watched my new crush. Perhaps not "watched" but "quietly appreciated his presence." During the next meal I brought my tray to meet him near the television, where he balked at political disagreements and reality TV shows. His cynicism was infectious and his eyes were friendly, framed by those damn, darling wrinkles that curved like a murder of crows.

My last few days in the hospital rounding out a two-week stay, I spent time with George, a hippie AcroYoga and tai chi fanatic, and Robert, a big older guy who hummed his daughter's favorite song while coloring pictures of suns with Crayola crayons. George gave me a book on Buddhism and astrology, and I gravitated toward the Buddhist concept of a no-self. "In Buddhism, the term anattā (Pali) or anāt-man (Sanskrit) refers to the doctrine of 'non-self,' that there is no unchanging, permanent self, soul or essence in living beings."[1] I figured if I was a nonself, then nothing in my life was fixed or permanent. Maybe I wouldn't lust after knives anymore. Maybe I wouldn't think of suicide every second of every day like I'd done for the last nine years. Maybe there would be hope for me.

1. Brian Morris, *Religion and Anthropology: A Critical Introduction* (Cambridge: Cambridge University Press, 2006), 51.

Later, I met Justin, a homeless thirty-year-old. He was a new patient in the unit. (People came and went like the changing seasons—fall and winter, MTV's *Real World: Paris* and *Real World: San Francisco*.) I remember Justin saying something in a group therapy session about the strength of the community in the hospital. Taken by his remarks, I sat with him while he ate lunch like Meredith did with me when I first arrived. Ironically, there was nothing worse than being alone while suicidal.

Justin and I continued to hang out after our "lovely" stay at CAC. I stole some of the small tubes of lotion—hey, it was a good leave-in conditioner—as if they were from a five-star hotel.

I boarded another ambulance and was wheeled out on a stretcher, cupping my hands to wave like the queen. I was transferred to Saint Gregory Hospital since CAC only permitted a two-week stay (to make room for the next batch of patient-inmates). At Saint Gregory Hospital, the ward was much smaller. Basement-like. I was hallucinating large black and shadowy monsters that resembled Dementors from *Harry Potter*. (I had always wanted to be a wizard.) Hiding behind sheets, rocking back and forth, teeth chattering, hands shaking, eyes twitching, I felt like I was having an orgasm gone seriously wrong. In this hospital I wasn't allowed to have my door closed, and the guards were like sharks circling their prey. I screamed whenever our eyes met and hid behind my navy hoodie.

There I met another new friend, Lacey, a college student with bipolar disorder. I was medicated out of my damn mind with Prolixin, a small seafoam-green pill that gave me tardive dyskinesia. The symptoms of tardive dyskinesia include random muscle movements in the tongue, arms, and legs. In severe cases, movements can affect breathing.

After leaving the hospital, Lacey would tell me, "You looked like a fucking zombie when we first met."

There wasn't much psych-ward romance in this hospital. I was pretty fucking pissed for the first week—which felt like years while locked in a building that consisted of a narrow hallway and two small rooms with screaming mental patients on too much decaf coffee and Adderall. My parents arrived during the allotted one-hour visit, and I shuffled to the cafeteria table like an inmate in shackles. My mom started crying like she always did, and my dad told her to chin up, be strong. A few tears ran down his face, and I thought to myself, *This is as bad as it gets.* I was faced with a big Nigerian man crying—one who would shout at *The Maury Show* when poverty-stricken women cried for their children who would grow up without fathers. He wiped away his tears.

Later Lacey and I met Sam, an older man with anger-management issues. He got hopped up on the decaf coffee like most patients; I swore the guards spiked it to watch us guinea pigs for medication trials as if we were contestants on *Big Brother*. We all shared what landed us in the hospital, going around the circle like inmates: "Whatcha in for?" The psych ward was a cross between a sleepaway camp and a supermax prison.

Because I was transferred from CAC to Saint Gregory and I didn't improve, my story remained the same: hallucinations and suicidal ideation. Pretty tame, a nonviolent "crime." I thought Sam might have tried to kill someone or at least assaulted a guy. I suspected there was more to his story from his coy explanation of his reasons for being there. Soon all the other people of color had been discharged from the hospital except for me, Lacey, and Sam, leaving us alone with a group of white soccer moms. Naturally the three of us became friends. "Chin up, be strong" wasn't a mantra reserved for me and my family. I realized that other people of color experienced the same erasure of their pain. The Strong Black Woman trope pressures other women (as well as men) to distance themselves from mental-health treatment.

We called ourselves the Brown Trio. We drew stick figures with matching leather jackets and pretended to be an edgy version of the Pink Ladies.

Among the drawings I did in the hospital was a slightly more detailed version of those Stickman games boys played in middle school, where they jumped around and killed other weaponized stick figures. Bodies overlapped with one another. I wrote a bad poem above the image in my composition notebook: *Sometimes I cannot explain what it is I have seen / tangled.*

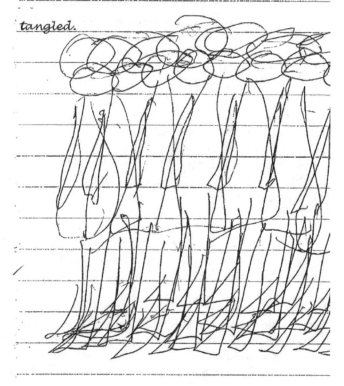

Freda Epum, *Sometimes I cannot explain what it is I have seen / tangled*, 2015. Image courtesy of Freda Epum.

The third time I went to the psych ward I was twenty-one years, eight months, and eight days old.

Two months after my first and second hospital-hotel-prison stays at CAC and Saint Gregory Hospital, I found myself in O'Henry Hospital. I was there for three weeks, my longest stay so far. Each day I met with Dr. Andrews, the therapist in the ward. I spent hours writing letters to a past self in my composition notebook, asking how I wound up in the same position again. This time it was a marijuana-induced hallucination, more shadows, more screams, more horror-like orgasms. Sex with the monster was exhausting, and he hadn't even bought me dinner yet.

Leading up to the hospital stay, things were more or less the same. I was still attending dialectical behavior therapy along with group therapy, which I got to do with my friends from the first hospital experience, Justin and Lacey. The community support group felt like an Alcoholics Anonymous meeting and a group interview combined.

"So, tell me a bit about yourself?"

"My name is Freda Epum. I recently graduated from Smith College in western Massachusetts where I studied studio art, American studies, and museum studies. My past experience includes working at my university's art museum for four years, serving as a communications assistant for a local arts nonprofit, and leading reading groups for third and fourth graders in inner-city schools. My skills include crying myself to sleep, crying myself awake, crying on bus rides, in bathrooms, on therapists' couches. Perhaps my biggest accomplishment would be spearheading a personal project, painting red-orange sunsets a stark baby-blue with my tears."

We then proceeded to list our diagnoses like bullet points on a resume.

"I'm struggling with:"

- Social Anxiety
- Psychotic Depression
- Complex PTSD
- Generalized Anxiety
- Panic Disorder with Agoraphobia

"Welcome, Freda."

Eventually my friends and I stopped going to the community support group, not because we were no longer in need of support but because support became, quite frankly, exhausting. Over the next few weeks, I continued to take my Effexor and Ativan and Trazodone and Geodon and Topamax and I slept and slept and slept. I hit the "apply" button on repeat, lines from my endless cover letters creating a poem of key points:

I am interested in pursuing an internship with the program
As a student, I began involving myself more in
Helped me to gain experience in
My abilities include
I believe my experience of over five years in
Would make me a strong and effective candidate
Throughout undergrad I held the position
In this role, I worked with
My research derives
In closing
I believe the position to be a great fit and
Look forward to following up with you
As you progress in the hiring process
If you need any additional information
Please don't hesitate to contact me

Over twenty cover letters and twenty resumes and twenty clicks on "apply" and twenty follow-up emails later, no one had been encouraged to contact me. Frustrated, I continued to research my medications. I hoped that, as a young faux scientist, I would find the cure to depression. I hoped to understand my illnesses to understand myself. In doing so, I found chemical reactions between Effexor, a serotonin and norephedrine antidepressant, and Geodon, a second-generation antipsychotic. Reactions often manifest as a series of adverse effects, such as continuous spasms and muscle contractions, motor restlessness, rigidity like Parkinson's, tremors, slowed movement, and tardive dyskinesia. They can also initiate serotonin syndrome or QT-interval prolongation, a dangerous racing heartbeat. Through some simple googling, my faux-scientist self could tell that these doctors had mis-prescribed my meds; I could identify the dangerous interactions between them. At the same time, my amateur sleuthing heightened my severe anxiety, the very symptom I was afraid of.

Later that night I sat in my closet filled with marijuana smoke, a towel stuffed in the crack between the floor and the bottom of the door to hide the smell from my parents. Many psychiatrists discourage smoking weed while taking medications. Pfft. My heart raced, or so I thought. My body felt weak, as if I was about to faint, or so I thought. I could die at any second from QT-interval prolongation, or so I thought. I sat there, unable to move for several hours, until my brother found me. I woke up with another nurse asking me if I was trying to commit suicide.

"Where do you see yourself in five years?"

In August 2016, I began to research new places to live with what little money I had saved working at the café. A caseworker told me supported housing would solve all my problems. Supported housing would help me move into an apartment staffed by community health centers and provide me with a paid position until I got back on my feet. Determined as ever, I called apartment listings every day. I was on a high dose of Adderall (an "antidepressant" for treatment-resistant depression) and I felt "fucking great!" I was either manic or high or both. I did not move into supported housing because the me from the first hospital reminded me that supported housing would pack mentally ill patients together like anchovies, like bodies in under-funded sick units, like in slave ships. Everything moved faster than it should have. It would smell, and the residents would scratch and shake with dysphoria like the patients detoxing from drugs whom I befriended in the unit.

○○○

The next month I went home and moved into my sister's room because I was afraid of the monstrous ghosts that roamed about in my bedroom, in closets, in alcoves, under the bed, and between the sheets. It felt better but not quite. Thanks to anti-anxiety pills and Adderall, I was slightly better at interviews. Soon after I was released from the first hospital stay (my joint vacation at CAC and Saint Gregory), I got my first job since graduating college. It was a customer service manager position at a food publication that ran editorials about self-cutting knives and refillable wine glasses and dancing rolling pins. We had a partnership with the makers of *Beauty and the Beast*.

I quit this job, then others. I went through jobs like summer flings, always searching for the one that would make me happy. My resume read Customer Service Manager, Ameri-Corps Member, Server, Job Coach Part One, Job Coach Part Two. A few interviews later, I fell sick again.

610 days later, I returned to O'Henry Hospital.

The fourth time I went to the psych ward I was twenty-three years, four months, and ten days old.

At this point Trump was about to be sworn in as president, and I was working as an independent contractor with an organization that served adults with developmental disabilities. My position was titled "Job Coach." But on my resume under BEHAVIORAL HEALTH AND EDUCATION EXPERIENCE, I listed the position as "Direct Support Professional," the way you dress up a casual outfit with lipstick and heels when you're really just a girl who wants to go home and take off her bra. I hated the job. I'd just quit my previous one ("Server, Cashier, and Professional Smoothie Maker") at Veggie Circle, which I acquired after the second hospital stay in the summer of 2016. I'd secured that job by being extra charming and lying that I was a vegan in my interview. (I chewed gum on my walk to work, fearing that a coworker might smell the ham-and-spinach omelet on my breath.)

It was ironic that I was a job coach when I couldn't find a job I wanted. After I left to find "new opportunities," I started a similar job where I taught small groups of adults with developmental disabilities a variety of subjects like painting and basic living skills, and, naturally, I developed the class How to Ace an Interview.

By this point I was quite good at interviews. Given the number of interviews I had, I eventually stopped crying before they began and was able to maintain eye contact for the socially appropriate amount of time.

My psychiatrist was about ready to give up. Nardil was one of the few medications I hadn't tried and was considered the "gold standard for treatment-resistant depression." The medication came with dietary restrictions like the inability to consume cheese because, you know, it would kill me. The medication had side effects similar to Adderall. I became manic, determined to get out of Tucson and dashing to plan a move to Ohio for a master's in creative writing. I was unsure it was what I wanted to do, dazed by failed jobs and precarious interviews. I was used to pain and scared of being alone.

A few weeks later I secured my spot in the master's program. Released from my last stay at hospital-prison-camp O'Henry, I spent most days roaming the desert in the summer heat, soaking up all the things I'd miss. In some ways I would miss even the interviews, even the "five-star" hospital hotels. I would miss who I'd become. I would miss what I'd overcome. I would miss myself.

In early fall, I walked past the sunsets, the colorful adobes, the cascading mountains, the cacti I ran into when I was five. I walked past the twenty-year-old in a navy blazer, orange blouse, and gray pencil skirt. I walked past the girl with red-tipped marker, white hospital gown, and composition notebook hoping to find a better self. I was off to Ohio.

One year into graduate school I'd struggle with the idea of going home to Arizona for the summer. The green in Ohio was alluring. White frat bros were made palatable when they coincided with nature. But I missed the adobes. I missed the mountains, the sprawling desert. I missed the days where someone would say, "Hi, how are you?" and I could actually respond with "Good, and you?" But memories of hospitals, Nameless Heroine's car accidents, verbal abuse, and heartbreak replayed in my mind. I read a diary entry of what I call a coping card: *You are different. You are strong for challenging yourself to do the things that scare you. Now breathe in and out of one nostril at a time.*

In *Slate*, Faylita Hicks writes about getting her MFA in creative writing only to work at an Amazon warehouse. A few years later I shared the story with my current partner, Mr. Zuckerberg, since it captured my deepest fears of failure compared to my successful, gainfully employed peers. I tried to make sense of all the hospitalizations and failed interviews. I wasn't strong like my friends and family wanted me to be. I was without hope, broken.

I'm no longer friends with any of the people I met in the psych wards and wonder where they are now. Despite my frequent hospitalizations and improvement at job interviews, I didn't truly get better until I moved to Ohio and was diagnosed with Bipolar Type 1 with Psychotic Features. It was there I had a fresh start and proper medication—mood stabilizers, not antidepressants since they make bipolar people unstable.

In *The Collected Schizophrenias*, Esmé Wang writes, "A capitalist society values productivity in its citizens above all else, and those with severe mental illness are much less likely to be productive in ways considered valuable: by adding to the cycle of production and profit."[2] I could not add to this cycle of production and profit. Though I had lived with my parents, I was broke, and after I moved out I was on food stamps and attended free mental-health clinics. If I did not produce for my hallucinated parents, snake-skinned mother and grossly unshaven father, I was doomed to die—to become an unemployed zombie.

2. Esmé Weijun Wang, *The Collected Schizophrenias* (Minneapolis: Graywolf Press, 2019), 51.

Years later, in a dream, I'm back at O'Henry Hospital. I enter my room after the nurses have me undress to check for sharp implements. The snake-skinned woman in red lipstick and grossly unshaven man return, she dressed in a black pantsuit and he in a brown blazer with navy slacks. I'm wearing nothing but army-green scrubs. The air smells sanitized and the floor feels cold and the pills taste like candy and the sky is no longer above us, the sky is neither a red-orange sunset nor a rainstorm dyed baby-blue with tears. They close the door behind them with a contract in hand and a freshly cleaned knife on a shiny silver platter.

I stand up and stretch my arms out, smiling.

"When can you start?"

The Meek Black Woman

I need to create an alter ego, The Meek Black Woman, to show you who I really am. My voice has always been timid, quiet, and at times nonexistent. To be soft-spoken is simply a predisposition, a natural mode of being. I often wonder how this disposition stands in contrast to The Angry Black Woman. What gives me the right to be angry beyond my difference (as if that weren't enough in itself)? I could use both my meekness and anger as sources of strength—I could scribble on random index cards: *You're different, and that's okay! You're beautiful no matter what!*

It's hard for me to believe these statements. After all, they were written by The Meek Black Woman.

The Meek Black Woman has no real convictions. She stands for nothing, at least not yet. She doesn't know that rage is resistance.

In *The Cultural Politics of Emotion*, Sara Ahmed states:

> Crucially, anger is not simply defined in relationship to a past, but as an opening up to the future. Being against something is also being for something, something that has yet to be articulated or is not yet.[1]

As Audre Lorde reminds us, anger is visionary. Lorde both contested and embraced the idea of The Angry Black Woman. She spoke passionately about the Black woman's right to be angry as long as her anger is productive. Lorde writes, "When focused with precision, [anger] can become a powerful source of energy serving progress and change."[2]

---

1. Sara Ahmed, *The Cultural Politics of Emotion* (Edinburgh: Edinburgh University Press, 2004), 175.
2. Audre Lorde, "The Uses of Anger," *Women's Studies Quarterly* 9, no. 3 (Fall 1981): 8.

Inside me was anger. I was angry that I was sick. I was angry that I lived in a world that stigmatized mental illness. I was angry that I would be dependent on medication my entire life. I was angry because of my difference. The rage inside was deafening.

After applying to MFA programs, I initially turned down my acceptance to my alma mater in Ohio. I was afraid of teaching. The opportunity to get paid to write didn't matter to me as soon as the reality of having to stand in front of a classroom and speak with authority settled in. After all, I was The Meek Black Woman.

I realized things were different during my third hospital stay at O'Henry. I couldn't stay in Tucson. I needed a job where I could make more than $12 an hour, or I needed to be able to write full-time.

Again I sought out treatment, hoping for a better outcome than the other times I entered a psychiatrist's office. It was fall in Ohio, and I was stressing over schoolwork. Stress often triggered a bout of depression and irritability. The school psychiatrist was an overbearing white man who relished the power of holding his patients' emotions in the palm of his hand.

He would tell me about all the things that were wrong with me—

mental illness, mental illness, mental illness, and mental illness some more.

When we first met, he pointed out our difference: "You're Black, and I'm white." He diagnosed me with Bipolar Type 1 with Psychotic Features and Generalized Anxiety. All I heard was

mental illness mental illness mental illness.

After my diagnosis, I didn't know how to feel. Should I be relieved that I finally figured out what was wrong with me? I'd been diagnosed with many other illnesses before—Psychotic Depression, Panic Disorder, Social Anxiety, Borderline Personality Disorder. I took medication after medication, but the rain cloud stuck with me. It wasn't until my bipolar diagnosis and a new cocktail of Lamictal, Trileptal, Buspar, and Perphenazine, that I began to feel like myself—whatever that meant. See, I had been depressed for so long that I wasn't sure who I was. General descriptors still seemed accurate—Nigerian American, artist, writer, forever mentally ill. It was the forever part that scared me. Though I'd been depressed, anxious, and irritable for as long as I could remember, there was still some part of me that thought, *This too shall pass*. She was wrong. Bipolar disorder has no cure. You manage it with therapy and medication. As I settled into my life in Ohio, I needed to accept this new reality and my intersectional identity—raced and disabled.

How can I redefine the narrative of "handicapped" (incomplete, defective, not whole, not as it should be) to allow myself to speak, to create visual likeness, or to simply be still? Govern my own autonomy and choose the negative space around and between notions of health and illness—finally feeling free.

The terms "neurovariant" and "neurotypical" changed how I look at the idea of disease. How easy and unfortunate it is to dismiss grief as mere feeling. How easy it is to dismiss feeling as unworthy of critical examination.

How soon will you be fixed? How long until you are no longer broken?

My notes read, *If you are not to be fixed, then what good are you?*

In 1970, a German activist group called the Socialist Patients' Collective recognized capitalism as the root cause of all illness. To be sick, then, was a political act: a passive resistance against capitalism. The group's slogan: "Turn illness into a weapon."[3] I knew that my illness marked my body, but it was more than that. It marked my voice too.

But suddenly I was no longer The Meek Black Woman. My illness made my voice deafening.

3. Socialist Patients' Collective, *SPK: Turn Illness into a Weapon* (Krrim Verlag Fur Krankheit, 1987).

179

MARKED MANIFESTO

> *I maintain unequivocally that there is such a thing
> as* marked *writing . . . the space that can serve as
> a springboard for subversive thought, the precur-
> sory movement of a transformation of social and
> cultural structures.*
> —Hélène Cixous, *"The Laugh of the Medusa"*[1]

There is nothing more revolutionary than to see and love
the sick. To feel the wound and be aware of its existence and
what feeds it. To love others as strongly as your infection
rages. No longer repressed, one is open to love, to the giving
process that is encounter. There is no longer the mask of
productivity, of functionality. All that's left are the fragile
open fissures of chronic suffering.

I have never seen a more radical love than in a community
that celebrates its wounded and heals itself from infection
through the language of compassion, understanding, and
acceptance. These tools were never given to the sick in
great abundance; we've had to fashion them by our own
rules, by creating our own supply.

Do not deny my wounds. Do not tolerate them. Do not make
isolated institutionalized space for them. Do not offer me
bandages whose price demands further cutting. I am a
multitude of wounds. A flesh-eating wound. I am festering.
Etched into the background of history, bleeding. My sores
are unbearable, but at their worst they make you uncomfortable because they're different from your own.

---

1. Hélène Cixous, "The Laugh of the Medusa," trans. Keith Cohen and
   Paula Cohen, *Signs* 1, no. 4 (Summer 1976): 879, https://www.jstor.
   org/stable/3173239.

You wear a facade that sanitizes you, a coating to replace skin and ease denial. Your mask sees wounds as deviance, an unexpected poison. You feed it and give it a name, many names. The names are all symptoms, a family of disorders. Handicaps, you call them. *Dis*/abilities, a term derived from an inability to function in a world that values production, exertion, efficiency.

I am not a machine. I am not fit for human consumption. Even if I tell you I do my best, well, my best will never be the same as yours; it never quite meets the designated criteria. I was never given these white masks that sustain you. I do not want one; I won't create one. I am learning to nurse myself. I am trying to be my own caretaker because I was never meant to survive.

Why do you want me alive when I speak of my horror as a flesh-eating monster? What do you gain from governing my survival? I move through a cycle of cages, each one designed to change the form of my wounds but not to erase them.

Drop these masks that shield us. I need a radical love where you touch my brown skin the way you hold a baby's hand for the first time.

Encounter me like your first true love, hold me like I smell familiar, like the scent of the only flower found during the apocalypse. This is the apocalypse, we are all zombies, each infected. Why do we run? Love me openly, broken bones or bedridden, debilitated by anxiety or losing touch with reality.

Freda Epum, *Diary of a Wet Cloud Series*, 2015.
Image courtesy of Freda Epum.

To feel the wound and be aware of its existence and what feeds it. To love others as strongly as your infection rages. We will be together, both festering and healing, because that is the only way we know how to live.

Love*Sick*

I'm sitting and watching *Get Out* in a dirty house on a musty gray couch with a computer screen too close to my face. I'm with a new boy, voice deep like a baritone, and when we get to the part where the country-club-esque Black guy has a nosebleed and attacks Daniel Kaluuya, he touches my inner thigh. How romantic. I hope that he will touch more than my inner thigh, but I know he'll be a nothing-but-heartache boy. I sigh and go back to watching Catherine Keener salivate at the prospect of cutting out Daniel Kaluuya's brain.

I have a complicated relationship to family holidays; the tension that engulfs me shakes my muscles to their core. Hugs are stippled by awkward beats of silence. "How have you been?" "Good." And then off to the next time we'll see each other, months later. I've always wanted to have a significant other to accompany me on holidays, to serve as a buffer and rub my back in circles, whispering "You'll be alright" in my ear. I whisper "You'll be alright" to one energetic puppy and one middle-aged dog, hoping they'll rub my back with their paws.

You fall in love with a boy and you tell him you've had enough.

You fall in love with a boy and he tells you he sees no future.

You fall in love with a boy and he tells you it'll be nothing but heartache.

You fall in love with a girl and you can't be certain if the love is true.

You're very very tired tired of falling falling in love.

You begin to fall in love with yourself and she says not yet.

During college, I sat in a seminar with a professor who had just published a book about Beyoncé. I was surrounded by women who intimidated me with their intelligence. The class was called Race and Love, and I thought, how ironic, for I was raced without love.

Last night my friends and I talked about boys (and girls) and our hopes and dreams for the future. I tell them about the It'll-Be-Nothing-but-Heartache Boy. About how my mental illness scared him away—leaving me the "crazy" ex-girlfriend that so many women are characterized as. Maybe it was that I was too broken. Not good enough, not worthy.

Maggie Nelson writes, "I want you to know, if you ever read this, there was a time when I would rather have had you by my side than any one of these words."[1]

Stephen Greenblatt says: "The treasured object exists not principally to be owned but to be viewed."[2]

I find myself wishing that the It'll-Be-Nothing-but-Heartache-Boy who slipped away would gaze upon my body—still broken but healing. At that moment I felt like a feminist fraud, for I would've accepted all the male gazes in the world if I could have had his. *Bad Feminist* by Roxane Gay pops up in my head. Bad Feminist, Wanting Feminist, Uneasy Feminist, Needy Feminist, Feminist in Love (with a boy—oh no!).

After I gave my college-era ex, Bony-Shoulder Boy, my copy of Audre Lorde's *Sister Outsider*, he said it seemed like "homework or something." My best friend told me she'd read anything that was important to me. I read an article about platonic love on Autostraddle. I learned about self-love like an intellectual. "Get it how you can," someone once told me.

1. Maggie Nelson, *Bluets* (Seattle: Wave Books, 2009), 95.
2. Stephen Greenblatt, "Resonance and Wonder," in *Exhibiting Cultures: The Poetics and Politics of Museum Display*, ed. Ivan Karp and Steven D. Lavine (Washington, DC: Smithsonian Institution Press, 1991), 52.

I've come to realize that I've shared my bed with boys who don't love me. I was not privy to this until I met a genuine love. I attached myself to past romances; I built relationships based on loneliness and dependence to make myself hurt less. It was fruitless. I was an empty basket of fruit.

Mr. Zuckerberg, the latest love of my life, is here to stay. We met during my first semester of graduate school. I am still preoccupied with past loves, but he is a nice distraction. He's strange, a white nerd topped with curls, afraid of commitment like me, who's not ready to let anyone in. Dependence is a close friend, but I want him near me, someone to quiet my mind. He has the sweetest periwinkle eyes. His height makes me feel small in his arms, protected. A feeling I did not know I needed until now. Eventually we grow closer. We cement our love for each other over meat lovers pizza, then a soft kiss before asking for companionship. As we walk hand in hand, I tuck his love safely away in my pocket. It is a mature infatuation, quiet, confirmed, passing relationship tests with flying colors. He reads me poetry sweetly and recognizes my pain without judgment. I am reminded of a past partner who said, "You're always sad." That is no longer a given. I am now cared for despite my pain.

Microprocessing: Bob Evans

I am sitting outside the diner in Ohio we wait for a table I am with a six-foot brunette boy blue eyes periwinkle soft boy with soft cushiony skin sits beside me closer and closer warm together I see other cushiony soft palevioletred cheeked pale dermises with hard looks not soft staring at us the brown dermis and cream dermis couple blending on the bench we go inside and I order chocolate-chip pancakes and he orders cinnamon hotcakes with warm syrup on the side there are more hard looks from saggy dermis folks and my pale other half stares back soft turned cold with disapproval I like to twirl my hair anxious so anxious a curl sticks out covered in warm soft syrup I eat it hoping to consume my anxiety digest my brownness but there's no use I wish I was vanilla frosting like cinnamon-covered pancakes like the cream dermis couple with the palevioletred cheeks

Microprocessing: Build a Baby

I'm with pale dermis boy and I tell him I want a baby build a baby I show my students build a baby contents they want the baby with the blue eyes bright hair bright skin bright baby I want a brown baby HTML color code #D2691E baby my baby's build defies the high price good health wishes or will my baby be a blue baby a baby with baby blues I want to build a baby construct my belly as a chamber of secrets as a safe a box I want to house my baby protect them from the others the highly engineered built babies baby 3000 I want to build a baby I want to tell her sweet sweet baby you're my sweet baby built by HTML color code #8B4513 my baby

~~violence happens to me when~~

I'm finally able to build a baby and she is beautiful she comes out of my HTML color code #A52A2A body and she is the most *beaut-tee-full* baby I have ever seen I build a whole website program all the colors shades of sienna make the most beautiful babies you've ever seen digital skins glowing

Microprocessing: Body Goes to the Movies

my heart is a place of solitude a   *pl-ay-sss* o' *sol-eh-2*   solitude house in my body in the body my body is a lonely entity
I take my body out on a date at the movies we see *Invasion of the Body Snatchers* Body snatches my hand and
suddenly I am holding hands with my soul case I like to
be intimate with Body hold Body bring my Body into the
cave of silence Body kisses me deep and slow she likes
to become a house in my organs a home to no-where the
empty   [empty]   movie theater inside me broken
bodies run in the family maybe one day you'll have one too

~~violence happens to me when~~

my body is broken yes but not empty she breaks because
she is full of all of the world's insistence that she is worthless she becomes a star in *Invasion of the Body Snatchers*
body makes seven figures now she jumps out from the
screen oh 3D oh IMAX she snatches the moviegoers and
bends each body in half one by one broken bodies run in
the family now you have one too

Microprocessing: flower shop

I really wanted that backpack from Everlane I really wanted those chestnut Chelsea boots from Nordstrom my mom really wanted that multicolored bag from Louis Vuitton I really wanted the Burberry perfume that smelled like roses the roses were soft and delicate I saw the bouquet of yellow roses at the flower shop but left because I really wanted these custom Adidas with the cheetah print and neon-green stripes I saw a boy with a T-shirt that just said "Three Stripes" and I knew I did not like the boy because he probably could buy those custom Adidas with the cheetah print and neon-green stripes and I could not I did not want to be the girl at the Halloween party with the orange yard-sale sweater I wanted to be one of the girls who wore patent-leather stilettos but I did not want to fall on my face and have to go to the emergency room because I did not have health insurance and still wanted to be able to buy that backpack from Everlane I thought I would find a cheaper prettier backpack so when I got off the plane I admired this girl's luggage she wore UGG boots so I knew it could not have been too much money but she must have been one of those rich white girls with the ponytails because when I got home to look up the price the backpack was $300

~~violence happens to me when~~

I finally bought my mom those yellow roses because they were soft and delicate like ponytails

The Aesthetics of Safety

In graduate school, I woke up one morning and lay in bed for another two hours. I got up, feeling the dirty, spongy carpet between my toes as I turned the channel to *House Hunters*, where a suburban mom was frustrated by her lack of granite countertops and marble backsplash. *We'll need to entirely gut this kitchen*. I walked past my kitchen with laminate countertops and a sticky floor. I questioned if being poor meant being so broke that you brushed your teeth with salt. I sighed and brushed my teeth with $2 Aim toothpaste—or was it $1.99? Every cent mattered.

It is 2020. I wake in the morning and turn the television on, pausing on *Flavor of Love*. I've been watching reruns of it the past week. In the first episode, Public Enemy's Flavor Flav knights his adoring fans and potential lovers with cheeky nicknames like "Smiley" and "New York," "Thing 1 and Thing 2" and "Goldie." I watch this episode for what might be the second or third time, years after its original airing. I imagine Flavor Flav draping a large clock around my neck. "Here you go, Cry-ee," he says before shouting, "Flavor Flav!"

Flavor Flav is a master of ceremonies, as am I. He's a hype man, someone who gets the crowd excited. Our similarities might end there.

After Mr. Zuckerberg and I moved in together in the summer of 2019, I found out he hates reality television. We are an odd match, considering MTV's *Laguna Beach* and Game Show Network's *Baggage* are among my favorite sick-day TV shows. He dislikes the voyeurism of watching others' strong and complex emotions on-screen. I am, for some reason, fine with it. But he loves Hawaiian pizza so clearly his taste is up for debate.

I wonder what it would be like to be on reality television. I imagine a room full of Black women, all of us crying. There would be think piece after think piece written about what should change about our society—the "thoughts and prayers" of the media world before we move on to the next news cycle. Though maybe the producers would be congregating in the corner.

"Did you catch that? This is gold."

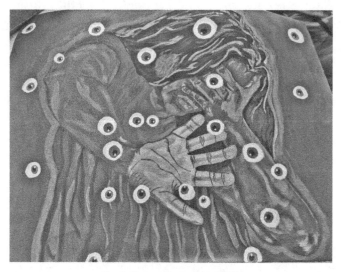

Freda Epum, *Protect Me*, 2011.
Image courtesy of Freda Epum.

In Heather Christle's *The Crying Book*, she writes, "People cry out of fatigue. But how horrible it is to hear someone say, 'she's just tired.' Tired, yes, certainly, but *just*? There's nothing just about it."[1]

I read Hanif Abdurraqib's poem "How Can Black People Write about Flowers at a Time Like This." I've always known what a time like this is: the latest illness, the failing economy, the police deaths, the stolen children. It isn't news to me. I disconnect myself from the insects that come to kill off my garden because I am tired. Audibly, visibly tired; I feel that someday this feeling will bury me. I think of Brittney C. Cooper and tiredness: "Tiredness might not be an emotion, but it is an affect. I feel it, I sense it, it exists on the surface of my skin and underneath, and it contours my relationships—political, professional, and personal."[2]

I was born out of tiredness. I was born tired. The tiredness felt navigating spaces as a person with intersecting identities: Black and woman. A lamentation is tiredness, as well as a deep-seated frustration.

There have been weeks on end when I wake up in the morning and say out loud to myself, speaking into the void, "I am tired." Fresh off the dopamine boost of a good workout session: "I am tired." Even if I am having a good day: "I am tired." I used to think that chronic fatigue syndrome could really be chronic Black girl syndrome. I breathe in tiredness and breathe out stress as many Black women do, statistically.

1. Heather Christle, *The Crying Book* (New York: Catapult, 2019).
2. Brittney C. Cooper, "Black Autumn: On Black Anger, Tiredness, and the Limits of Self-Care," in *The Crunk Feminist Collection*, ed. Brittney C. Cooper, Susana M. Morris, and Robin M. Boylorn (New York: Feminist Press, 2017), 315.

Flavor Flav would nickname me "Cry-ee" because the last five years have been my Crying Years. By that I mean to say it has been a period of five years in which I have cried more than ever before.

I learned that crying in front of medical professionals means nothing.

I imagine them after our appointment, backs turned in the corner, watching hidden-camera footage: "Did you get that? This is gold."

In writing, I often try to blend reality (nonfiction) with what I think of as hyper-reality (speculative nonfiction). If one is less inclined to listen to my real-life pain, then why not allow an imaginary monster to speak for me? Why not let the dead flowers speak to my own affect or, perhaps, my own fate?

Right now there is a phantom virus outside, most affectionately known as The 'Rona. It's funny that when I first saw the words "The 'Rona," it was on-screen (where most of my life lives these days). It reminds me of the meme with a frayed-looking Muppet next to text that reads, "When you feel a little tickle in your throat." Mr. Muppet's eyes go wide, and he clutches his invisible pearls. "Is that The 'Rona?!" Mr. Muppet looks around, eyes shifting.

Every other day I have some sort of existential anxiety moment thinking about whether I would be offered a ventilator or not in the event of a hospital overload. Whether I would die alone inside a cold room and if I'd be lucky enough to see my loved ones on an iPad wrapped in plastic, a haunting metaphor of what I, too, could become: an inanimate object, carefully covered.

Saying "The 'Rona" lessens the impact of "coronavirus" or the even more clinically chilling "COVID-19." 'Rona leans on your counter shedding herself, and you might go, *Oh, that's just 'Rona again! Doing what she does best*, as if you're in the latest postapocalyptic sitcom. COVID-19 sheds, and you think of your loved ones clutching their chests as each respiratory droplet flutters to the ground. Mr. Zuckerberg and I are talking about adopting a dog because we need another life form around, maybe naming her 'Rona. We think out loud about the collective trauma experienced across the globe. With our new puppy 'Rona, perhaps we would be just like those watching the latest quarantine movies on Netflix, inviting the darkness in to come and play.

I am doing things quietly these days, methodically, savoring what might be the last few times I wrap my hair at night, moisturize my face, water my plants, sweep the floors. They are all domestic things to reinforce the idea that "I am safe here." Living on my own, with Mr. Zuckerberg, safe from my childhood traumas. It is a new experience for me. Nearly agoraphobic during the Crying Years, I stayed inside because I was fearful of what the outside world could do to me, as if there were a million little viruses in the wind, in the people, in the very ground of the Earth itself. It was never because I felt safer inside. Inside I was alone with myself in my own brain, where there, too, were a million little viruses. I would need to wrap the fleshy-pink-brain-matter couch in my head in plastic. Wrap the whole of my insides in plastic—only then would I be safe.

It's a shame that the outside now threatens not just my mind but my body. I want my body to feel safe. I want my body to be here tomorrow, a month from now, a year from now, for the foreseeable future. I would not have said the same thing five years ago. I did not want to wake up to see the new day in my Clorox wipe–resistant brain.

After Breonna Taylor, I search Instagram for home decor. Usually this is soothing. The sectional reminds me of comfort; the reading chair, security; the planters, protection. A few nights ago, I cried myself to sleep in my Mr. Zuckerberg's arms thinking about Breonna. She was young, respected as an EMT; she was beautiful, and she saved people when they were sick. When she was alive, she offered others safety. But when I look at photographs of her now, I see her ghost and my legs feel leaden again. I no longer feel safety in my home. I feel terror. I explain to my white partner that I worry someone will break into our home and kill me in my sleep. I tell him I want to get a gun. I used to have a pink Taser that I lost after moving. I imagine it in my hands—bright, solid, and powerful. Right now I would be honored to hold its beauty, breathe in its aesthetic. For once maybe have a role in my own freedom, or at least the impression of it. I began telling you, reader, about my tears, about my new name Cry-ee. This nickname was meant to describe my state of mind. Now I cry for justice. I cry for safety.

I want to write about the yellow roses or the sparkling violets or the stunning marigolds that Hanif Abdurraqib speaks of in "How Can Black People Write about Flowers at a Time Like This." I want blossoms to be in my future. I imagine covering a row of bouquets in Flavor Flav clocks to show that even though they are temporary, like the love between reality television show stars, they are still beautiful. I cannot water these flowers with my tears. My eyes are deserts now. They flutter shut at night, drained from the day. In the morning I pick a measly bunch of sunflowers at the supermarket. I want to write about the flowers, but it's painful to know we can never be friends. They'll just die again and again. "A time like this" is the longest relationship I've ever had. When I fall asleep, I know I will wake to the darkness. Once a month I might pick a flower from the neighbor's bushes. I'll take it home, water it, and nurture it the only way I know how. Soon "a time like this" will come knocking at the door and I'll say goodbye to my new friend—blowing away hope, till next time.

I now can definitively point to my desire for an aesthetic of safety. A consolation prize for the real thing—freedom—unattainable for Black people in American society. I find beauty in being protected from danger. I want to bottle up a perfume with scents like "whisper of freedom from hurt" combined with a "splash of security."

The hardest thing about being with my partner is not our difference; it's the grief. He will never truly know what it's like to grieve collectively and yet still feel devastating loneliness. I talk to my Black colleagues, friends, and family, and we say so much with our bodies. Right now, due to social distancing, there are Zoom meetings with the topic "Let's Be Alone Together." I think about how that's what Blackness feels like—the hysteria of doubting your own experience, the specter of death. We are the loneliest when we die.

Recently I planted my first lily in our backyard. It's begun to sprout. Soon I'll bring the flowers inside, the blossoms, the lilies, the violets, breathe in their fresh scents. I'll place them safely against the vintage mirror frame near the decorative fireplace—bringing beauty to my insides at long last.

"Why (I Choose to Remember)"
by Big Freda

At the Chinese buffet, I would sit in a scuffed leather booth, my pink light-up shoes dangling. There was a bright yellow goldfish swimming in a tank and a friendly server who usually remembered our family. Lo mein is one of my favorite foods, and I grabbed a big plate of it from the buffet aisle. My dad would sometimes fill two plates while my mom was a more modest eater. I believe that the restaurant has since closed down, but it's still dear to me. It's a simple memory, one where I don't quite remember the details of what happened except for the feeling of being happy and full.

While slurping down salty noodles, I would forget who I am. I am merely a daughter, a sister. I forget my Black girl body, my precarious mental state, my identity as both foreign and not foreign. I finish my plate, twirling the last bit of vegetables.

I've been thinking a lot about fragments and forgetting. In *Tender Points*, Amy Berkowitz writes, "The story of my pain is not an easy story to tell. Trauma is nonlinear. There are flashbacks and flash-forwards. And my story is a story about forgetting."[1]

I have grown older. My Black girl body is now a Black woman's body with the curves to prove it. I no longer have a beaten-up booth or a kind establishment to shield me from the realities of racism, the stigma of illness, or my painful attempts to claim a homeland.

---

1. Amy Berkowitz, *Tender Points* (Oakland: Timeless, Infinite Light, 2015; New York: Nightboat Books, 2019), 45.

In Childish Gambino's "Bonfire," he raps about the cliché of Black actors often becoming rappers.

I too have wondered whether my work would fit into a cliché. Not about rappers (though I secretly wish that I'd come up with the rap name Big Freedia first) but about Black writers, African writers. Will readers think to themselves, *Man, why does every African writer gotta write about family?* In some ways, the question feels childish (pun intended).

As a kid I used to sit down for my mother to do my hair. She would always ask, "Free, don't you want to look pretty?"

"Why?"

I was enthralled with the whys. Why was I obsessed with family? With race? With illness? With HGTV and the twins from *Property Brothers*?

I was searching for something not in the depths of Drew or Jonathan Scott's beards, but in my obsession with house hunting, with interior design. *I was searching for home.*

With all my whys, I longed for more than duality. I was against binaries so much that I had the phrase "both/and" tattooed on my left wrist. The tattoo was a constant reminder that I contain multitudes. I was more than my disorders. I was both/and.

While teaching in graduate school, I began my creative nonfiction class by writing "TRUTH" in big letters on the whiteboard. "What is it and why is it important in nonfiction?" I asked my students, my eyes wavering. "Is it possible that there can be multiple truths?" They nodded, twenty-year-old bobbleheads in sweatpants.

In "The Lifespan of a Fact," infamous for its feigned "true story," John D'Agata writes about a real boy who died by suicide in Las Vegas, but he changes certain facts, such as how the boy killed himself. When asked in an interview about why he chose to embellish, lie, or omit a fact, D'Agata simply said that it fit what the story needed.[2]

I've asked myself what the story of my life needs to feel complete. It would be a lie of omission to say that I'm now in the same place as I was when I began.

In Jennifer Lunden's "Evidence, in Track Changes," she writes: "It was a strange thing, editing my mother. Particularly since for my entire childhood, especially the first eleven years, she edited me." "Evidence, in Track Changes" is a new version of an earlier essay, "Evidence," about Lunden and her mother's fraught relationship. In the new version, Lunden's mother voices her perspective, adding track changes and comments in the margins of the essay. Lunden writes, "I didn't plan to edit her truth."[3]

2. Jennifer B. McDonald, "In the Details," review of *The Lifespan of a Fact*, by John D'Agata and Jim Fingal, *New York Times*, February 21, 2012, https://www.nytimes.com/2012/02/26/books/review/the-lifespan-of-a-fact-by-john-dagata-and-jim-fingal.html.
3. Jennifer Lunden and DeAnna Satre, "Evidence, in Track Changes," *DIAGRAM* 17, no. 3 (2017): 1, https://thediagram.com/17_3/lunden.html.

Who was I to write or even edit the story of my family? Why am I attempting to articulate their truths? I write about hybridity, about multiples, about being doubled. I write toward more than either/or, and I've now extended that approach to my relationships.

Writer Anne Lamott has said: "You own everything that happened to you. Tell your stories. If people wanted you to write warmly about them, they should have behaved better."[4]

Should have behaved better. My therapist once scolded me for my shoulds. He called it "shoulding," chuckling to himself. I embrace "tell your stories" but shy away from the shoulds like they're bad Chipotle burritos. Belief is what I wanted from others. I wanted to be believed about the monsters I saw, about the racism I've experienced, about never feeling truly at home anywhere.

Now, belief is what I extend to others. Belief that they are trying their best.

4. Anne Lamott, *Bird by Bird* (New York: Vintage Books, 1995).

As I sit in my parents' dining room, I look through old records and family photo albums. Photographs are our truest form of memory, "a way of imprisoning reality."[5] These photos—locked in the same cabinet as Stevie Wonder, Peter Tosh, and Marvin Gaye records—sing to me sweetly. The soundtrack allows me to remember nose kisses between my mother and me before I boarded a flight and left home for the first time. Chinese buffets with my boastful dad as he scarfed down three plates of food and I smirked in amusement. A talk show I performed with my sister in front of the bathroom mirror. My eldest brother's renditions of our favorite Usher songs. My soft grin as my other brother jammed to J. Cole.

My reality shares the same cell with others. More imprisoned realities. My Reality is dressed in orange, peeing in the toilet in front of others. Is she happy? My Reality is a dead Poussey from *Orange Is the New Black*, her memorial service held in the library, her favorite place. She's surrounded by many other truths, many other realities, *both* long cherished *and* long scarred.

I wish I could write a story about the sweet songs of loved ones as vividly as Hanif Abdurraqib. His memories are detailed, all-encompassing. They envelop us in Chance the Rapper's #blackboyjoy or stomach flutters during a first date at a Carly Rae Jepsen concert. But my memories are less intact; they exist in fragments, in episodes.

5. Susan Sontag, *On Photography* (New York: Farrar, Straus & Giroux, 1977), 163.

I put together the Greatest Hits of My Life. It has ballads, feel-good Top 40 hits, emo songs. I play it alongside the photos of my siblings and me as kids, piled on a couch with giggling faces that perfectly fit the frame.

In a dream, I am dressed in baggy sour-orange garb. I start a prison riot. Let all the imprisoned realities of the past roam free. In the background, "Visions" by Stevie Wonder coos and the multiple realities belt out in harmony.

Upon our escape from the penitentiary, My Reality and I write in graffiti: *The world is all about memory. What your mind chooses to remember and what you choose to forget.*

What does it mean to hold on to the sweetness of the past? I don't remember the last time we took a family photo. But if I were to capture us now, I'd put on some '80s R&B in the background. Play Earth, Wind & Fire and breathe in their sounds. Blend music with memory. Then lock them away and swallow the key.

Home (Body)

In *The Crying Book*, Heather Christle writes:

> I hear myself describe the intensity of tears, myself
> sobbing on the kitchen floor for no reason, "like a
> madwoman." Why "like"? In these moments I am
> one. I am. "Rose is a rose is a rose."[1]

These words appear near the end of her book, the time
when the reader goes *mmm* and closes the text, satisfied.

I, too, have held the identity of a "madwoman."

I have sobbed the uncontrollable salty streams of a
madwoman in an institution, in a bedroom.

I have shed a tear because
I have no home in a country
This leads to another because
I have no home in a mind
Which leads to another because
I have no home in a body.

A tear is a tear is a tear.

Add them together and you create a no-place, no-where
identity.

I still shed tears but also flash a small smile now. A tear +
a smile = a human. I've reconstructed myself into a human,
laid bare the soul of a teary-eyed Black girl with upturned
lips. This new human has found a place, slowly, quietly.

1. Heather Christle, *The Crying Book* (New York: Catapult, 2019).

HOUSEWARMING

When I think of *House Hunters*, there is always a trade-off between your wish list and what you are able to have.

Mr. Zuckerberg notes to me that it is so interesting how looking at apartments calms me down whereas it stresses him out. I tell him it's because I see all the possibilities of who you could be in that place. Perhaps I am searching for a different version of myself. I look for the same things now—dishwasher, bathtub, outdoor space, square footage. Dishwasher so my overwhelming anxiety and chronic pain (which I tell myself is laziness) doesn't stop me from having a fruit-fly-infested home, which my best friend of thirteen years tells me I've had in every living space prior. Bathtub to soothe my aching muscles and cleanse away days I replay in my head that could have been better. Outdoor space and square footage so I am not enclosed with my own thoughts.

When I look at apartments, I like to imagine myself there. I've been looking at apartments in Lagos, Nigeria for fun. I explore the neighborhoods Lekki and Yaba. I figure out which place would be closest to my fictional favorite shops, the grocery store, maybe a museum. I am enthralled by the possibilities. I look for the contact number to book a showing as if I could fly six thousand miles overnight. There I'd meet my new landlord, pay my deposit in naira, and accept my keys.

Possibilities, to me, signal hope, longing. In this list I want to write "future," but I stop myself. Possibilities, to me, are not postcards, long-distance Zoom chats, coordinating time zones, being reminded of a Facebook memory, listening to the same song in two different locations while having the same warm feeling. In my future, I want home, I want regular, consistent, steady, familiar, *close*. Who we are is who we've been is who we could be. I am an amalgamation of possibilities. An endless supply of what ifs, could bes, and should have beens.

When I think of my African heritage, I hear "should have been." Should have been better, closer to the ideal, closer to tradition. When I think of the story of my parents, I think of "could be." *What could be if sacrifice was not at the center? Who would they and I have been*?

Today, I have selected three apartments that I chose in my own very special episode of *House Hunters*. Other names for these homes are What If, Could Be, and Should Have Been.

As I near the end of this house hunt my stomach feels queasy—naked and raw, I've vomited my confessions. In *The Night Parade*, Jami Nakamura Lin writes, "I thought I would feel a rapturous moment of completion. *It is over.* Instead, I know it is done because I can no longer sit in it without breaking. I am spent."[1]

Many years have passed since my regular wakings to the red desert soil. I sit curled up in a muted gray IKEA reading chair in Ohio, back sinking into the throw pillow meant to conceal the too-stiff frame—crying alone in my apartment, mind thick with memory.

It is now 2023. My father is sick. On a Thanksgiving trip to Tucson where kin two-step to Burna Boy, I show these pages to my father as he lies in a hospital bed. "I need a heart transplant or else I will have eighteen months to live," he tells me over the phone while I am at a work function in Cleveland. His voice is dry with normalcy but his pauses smell like fear.

I want to tell you I feel helpless because that feels like the appropriate emotion. I do. I am no stranger to powerlessness. But mostly I feel like a coward. Too afraid to share a decade of anxieties, obsessions, sorrows with my parents— my mirror.

After reading my manuscript, my father texted me a long message ending with "I'm sorry for all the pains."

1. Jami Nakamura Lin, *The Night Parade* (New York: HarperCollins, 2023).

My mind leaped from the crying emojis I sent to my cousin Dumebi after reading my dad's heartfelt response to a page in *This Is the Place: Women Writing About Home*: "The word *home* is, for me, tied to the word *land*—home, homeland. Like many immigrants, I hold simultaneously two images of home: one feels transient and impermanent even though my family has resided here for forty years, and the other is, by now, almost entirely an imagined construct."[2]

My images of home, too, are fleeting. They are collages of West African sculptures on mantels, smiling brown babies framed on popcorn-textured walls, hecklings to rude short-haired dogs from pit bull to beagle, smoky scents of bubbling tomato paste, creaky joints dropping it low to Afrobeats. These images have no fixed location, but they make up my homeplace. bell hooks writes of this concept of "homeplace": "Despite the brutal reality of racial apartheid, of domination, one's homeplace was the one site where one could freely confront the issue of humanization, where one could resist."[3]

2. Hasanthika Sirisena, "Of Pallu and Pottu," in *This Is the Place: Women Writing About Home*, ed. Margot Kahn and Kelly McMasters (New York: Seal Press, 2017), 229.
3. bell hooks, "Homeplace: A Site of Resistance," in *Yearning: Race, Gender, and Cultural Politics* (Boston: South End Press, 1990), 42.

I bounce through time and memory, feelings of helplessness and shame, to tell you that there is no easy resolution here. In the end there is only the space I have crafted for myself through this narrative. The piecing together of emotion that has lent itself to a full picture of a human. And in the braiding, I've made myself a place.

What is it like to relax on a couch when you can't relax about racism? What is it like to spend so much time in bed due to illness? What is it like to look out a window and not see yourself outside?

After a few months, I decide on another home: the Comfortably Content Cottage. I set the table with yellow place mats (my afternoons are bright these days), straighten out my welcome rug, pour a calming cup of tea. I'm domestic now. Safe. I host a dinner party with scholars, artists, and poets. I've invited you as my special guest.

"Where have you been?" you ask.

I smile, excited to tell you my story.

In my home I am a human with a spider plant, hardwood floors, and a kitchen island.

In my home I am a human with a vintage rug, a mahogany bookcase, and lace curtains. The curtains frame the window with a view that shifts from Nigeria to Arizona to Ohio.

In my home I am a human who finally has her dream couch—plush, soft, and adorned with fluffy accent pillows and a basket full of throw blankets. I am a basket full of softness now.

I am soft.

In my home I am a human with a deep soaker tub and lit candles. Their vanilla scents fill the air.

In my home   I am a human.

I open the door and happily greet MTV.

"Welcome to my crib," I beam.

Acknowledgments

A book is always written in community, and my story is no different. So many people deserve a thank-you, though these individuals and institutions are particularly close to my heart.

Thank you to everyone who has laid eyes on this book and provided helpful feedback in any capacity, especially: Daisy Hernández, Cathy Wagner, cris cheek, TaraShea Nesbit, Paul Vogel, Louisa Pavlik, Heba Hayek, Carrie Bindschadler, Johnny Fuentes, Savannah Trent, Jen Sammons, Dylan Ecker, Kyle Flemings, Sam Gutelle, Kyle Swensen, Leah Christianson, Amy Mitchell, Matt Boyarsky, Trevor Root, Athena Dixon, Aditi Kini, Elissa Washuta, Cinelle Barnes, Kay Ulanday Barrett, Samiya Bashir, Edgar Gomez, and Erica Berry. I am fortunate to have a community of writers like you.

Thank you to my agent, Reiko Davis, for championing this book to the finish line. The phone calls, Zoom calls, edits, managing my anxiety. Reiko, you are everything I could have ever asked for in a publishing partner.

Thank you to my editors, Lauren Rosemary Hook, Kameel Mir, Margot Atwell. Thank you, Lauren, for believing in this weird little book so much and reigniting my confidence in my writing. Lauren, truly thank you for taking a chance on me. Thank you, Kameel, for your keen attention to detail, intentionality, and the deeper meaning of my book. Thank you, Margot, for your dedication to Feminist Press, a much-needed refuge in book publishing. Thank you to the entire team at Feminist Press, from publicity to cover design. Thank you for allowing my words to reach readers.

Thank you to the following for providing institutional support: Tin House Workshop, Miami University, VONA, Ragdale, Anderson Center, Lambda Literary.

Thank you to the following for publishing essays from this collection: Electric Literature, *The Rumpus*, *Heavy Feather Review*, *Rogue Agent*, *Nat. Brut*, *Bending Genres*, *Third Coast*, *Iron Horse Literary Review*.

Thank you to my therapist, Dr. Ritch Hall, for truly seeing me and always reminding me what I am capable of, creating a safe and culturally competent space to process my intergenerational trauma, and keeping me alive throughout my twenties and early thirties. Even when I felt alone, I could always turn to you.

Thank you to my closest friends for believing in me when I didn't think anyone else did, including encouraging me just to finish the damn thing, especially: Sol Kim, Brice Mickey, Ashley Swinford, Scarlett Chang, and Connor Hair. Thank you in particular to Sol Kim, my bestie since I was seventeen years old. We've grown up together as artists, BFFs, and sisters. There are no words to quantify how much of a support you've been during every pivotal moment in my adult life. I love you.

Thank you to my siblings for your unconditional love. Even as we took different paths in life and we lost our way, we always returned to each other. When I am at my lowest, you have always been my refuge from a harsh world and just a call away.

A special thank-you to my parents, especially my dad who always told me, "I wish I could write like you." Thank you, Daddy, for your endless confidence in me. Thank you, Mommy, for your tender love.

Thank you to the love of my life, Matthew Birkenhauer, for your thought partnership, editing skills, endless praise, sitting with me while I cried over this book, for your unwavering faith that this book would be published. You are the best thing that's ever happened to me. More than anyone else, our time together has helped me heal. Bubba, I learned to love myself through falling in love with you.

Thank you all.

FREDA EPUM is a Nigerian American writer and artist. She is the author of two chapbooks, *Input/Output* and *Entryways into memories that might assemble me*, which won the Iron Horse Literary Review Chapbook Competition. She is the cocreator of the Black American Tree Project, an interactive workshop about the legacies of slavery in American society. Epum's work has been published in *The Rumpus*, Electric Literature, *Vol 1. Brooklyn*, *Entropy*, *Bending Genres*, and others. She received her MFA from Miami University in Oxford, Ohio. Originally from Tucson, she now lives in Cincinnati.